Joshua
Out of the Desert

Beckie-Jo Snell

Strategic Book Group

Strategic Book Group
P.O. Box 333
Durham CT 06422
www.StrategicBookClub.com

ISBN:978-1-60911-926-3

Dedication

For my granddad Leslie Browne (1931–2008). Thank you for being such an encouragement to me and for being the world's funniest Scrabble player. Your laughter and sense of fun made my life richer and I am blessed to have been your granddaughter.

And for Andrew Benfield (1968–2008) a man of such courage and strength.

For Julz and Christopher, you are amazing and I feel so privileged to share your journey. *'For the Lord himself will come down from heaven, with a loud command, with the voice of the archangel and with the trumpet call of God, and the dead in Christ will rise first. After that, we who are still alive and are left will be caught up together with them in the clouds to meet the Lord in the air. And so we will be with the Lord forever'* (1 Thessalonians 4: 16–17).

And for Rose, it is truly my blessing to be your handmaiden; you are a woman of such grace and anointing, and I have learned so much from you. Thank you for walking with me through the desert and out of the other side, for laughing and crying with me, for holding my hands up when I couldn't lift them, and for speaking in the truth of the word of God. My sister you are truly a beautiful blessing.

Contents

Acknowledgments

So many people have come alongside me and encouraged me that it is hard to know where to begin, but I want to spend a few moments saying thank you.

Katy Allen, you are awesome and you have helped and blessed me so much. Thank you for encouraging me to be a woman of the word and a woman of prophesy.

Ian, thank you for standing with me and reminding me that 'there is no panic in heaven, only plans.'

Amber, thank you for putting up with me during the writing of this book, even when the pen drive went missing!

For Liz because 'we are overcomers who choose to overcome.'

For Jayjay because we are living in our miracles.

For Helen, Jim, and Mads for allowing a crazy houseguest to invade your space.

For Arran who assured me that 'somewhere there is somebody who is looking for a book just like mine.'

And for everyone at Kings Community Church, Lancaster, England. I am so blessed to be a part of you; this book exists because you stand with me.

INTRODUCTION

An Ordinary Life That Became Extraordinary

"It is time to be a people that recapture our dreams; it's time to come alive to the promises of God given to our generation. It's time to declare—as Joshua did, that, "Me and my household, we will serve the Lord."[1] It is time to come out of the desert."

At the start of this book I invite you to come with me on a journey and look at the life of an extraordinary man, walk his journey with him, and allow yourself to be challenged and inspired to walk with God in a new way. Joshua was a man who saw amazing things, yet he knew amazing hardship. This book looks at the young man who knew the pain of a captive childhood, the agony of a wilderness journey and also the awe of standing on the mountain with Moses. Joshua was a man with a heart, a man who worshipped with passion and who walked with obedience. His was often a lonely path; he knew the grief of seeing his generation and family die in nonbelief when they failed to catch ahold of what God was doing. Out of a multitude Joshua was one of two people to survive the wilderness journey and know the victory of crossing into the Promised Land. As we look at Joshua's life and glean from his experience, we will be inspired to move out of the desert.

We are good at wanting the experience. We want to see the water of our circumstances pile up and be held by the hand of God, but are we really prepared for the cost? Are we ready

---

[1]*Joshua 24: 15b*

to be found in the tent worshipping when everybody else has gone, to look at enemy territory and see the promise of a God who declares, *"This is holy ground."*?

How can we walk in difficult circumstances? How can we draw near to God? How can we be a people of integrity? How can we love out of the desert place? My prayer is that as you read this book alongside the scripture for each chapter you will be both challenged and blessed as you apply 'Joshua principles' to your life, principles of heaven that change earth.

It is time to be a nation of Joshua's—men and women who declare the plans and purposes of God with their worship, with their words, with their actions, and with their hearts. It is time to be excited, to live on the edge again.

Come with me on a journey . . .

CHAPTER 1

A Captive Childhood

"From birth I was cast upon you, from my mother's womb you have been my God. Do not be far from me, for trouble is near and there is no-one to help."
Psalm 22: 11

Some time ago I was leading a youth session and looking at heroes from the Bible, great men and women of God who had been used powerfully. Their testimonies were awesome—Saul, a man who defended genocide against Christians, who was blasted by God on a road, became blind, was healed, and then became an evangelist, an apostle and a scripture writer: Moses, the murderer, who ran away and hid, encountered the voice of God in a burning bush that didn't burn, and, despite a speech impediment, led the Jews out of Egypt, watching Pharaoh's vast army drown in the process. David, the adulterer, who arranged the murder of one of his own soldiers, was confronted by the prophet Nathan and repented, and became known as a man after God's own heart. Peter, who denied he even knew Jesus, spoke before he thought and sometimes seemed to miss the point, became a spirit-filled preacher who saw three thousand people saved at one meeting.

But as I looked at Joshua's life, he seemed different somehow. On the surface he didn't have the *powerhouse* testimony of these mighty men. His walk seemed a quieter walk. Then, as I looked closer, I realised that this wasn't a *quiet testimony*, this was a man who saw walls fall (Joshua 5), waters pile up in a heap (Joshua 3), and the sun stand still (Joshua 10). This was a man who asked God to stop time and

God did. This was a man who lived daily in the power and anointing of God.

It is good to look at the powerhouse testimonies of men and women of the Bible and see how God used them. It is good to know that God will overcome and will turn things around, but we must never forget that these mistakes came also with a tremendous cost. For Moses the cost of his temper was that he never crossed into the Promised Land. For David the cost of his adultery was that he lost his child.

Joshua was a man who lived among anger and disappointment; he saw the cost that Moses paid and determined in his heart to live differently.

Looking closer still at Joshua, you realise that this was a man who hadn't had it easy. This was a man who had grown up in the shadow of infanticide, slavery, and hard labour; a man who lived with a people overshadowed with disappointment and bitterness, who, even after they had freedom, remained expectant of disaster. Joshua was a man who spent the prime years of his life wandering in a desert because his family and friends chose to disobey God. This was a man who saw his family perish, and one who decided, as a young man, to take on a position of isolation to understudy the servant of God. Throughout his leadership, he was tested and tried but brought to Israel the peace and stability of God.

Sometimes we have a tendency in our culture to glamorise our mistakes, to let our mistakes dominate our testimony. Our confession becomes *this is what I was* as opposed to *this is who I am*. Don't get me wrong, God uses our mistakes and in his grace and mercy brings us back, but these things should never be the focus of our testimony. Our testimony is about who we are in God, not what we were before God. Our testimony is about what God is doing and what he will do. We rejoice in what God has done, in where he has brought us, but look for the next thing and the new things for today. The hallmarks of Joshua's life were not his childhood, his wilderness experience, or his battle with disappointment. Joshua is remembered as a man who stayed in the tent worshipping, as a man who marched around the walls of Jericho, and as a man who settled Israel in the Promised Land.

I believe we remember these things about Joshua because that was what he saw himself. He lived in the belief that God would do and that he was hearing God. There was no place in Joshua's thinking to doubt—he knew that there were enough people around him who would do that for him. Joshua found his identity in God and then in that identity, lived in his circumstance. It is too easy sometimes to live in the circumstance and then try and fit God in or find God in it. God wants to show us who we are first in order that we impact our circumstances with His kingdom power displayed through our lives.

Joshua understood that the confession—*'from my mother's womb you have been my God'* was not a confession of despair but of hope. You have been my God not because things were so terrible that there was no option, but because in your grace you carried me. You have been my God because you always knew that there was a plan and that it would be better.

Growing up for Joshua wasn't easy—he was born into a position of slavery and captivity. Some years before Joshua's birth, Pharaoh had ordered the murder of all young boys under the age of two. Most of them were drowned in the Nile, but Moses was the exception. Joshua grew up in the shadow of this—of the knowledge that this could happen again. Imagine the terror of a mother giving birth to a baby boy and knowing what had happened before—these are women who would have watched the drowning of young babies—maybe their own brothers—years before. As soon as he was old enough, Joshua would have been pressed into hard labour, building massive constructions for Pharaoh or making bricks with limited resources. These were not pleasant jobs, and I imagine the workers were not given huge amounts of respite.

I wonder how much Joshua heard of Torah, of God, of worship in this time; I wonder if he heard at all. Moses changed

Joshua's name from Hoshea. Hoshea means salvation[2], which to me indicates that at some stage Joshua's parents must have had hope or revelation that someday things would be different. I wonder if Joshua himself ever wondered at the meaning of his name, if he ever went to God with his name and said 'what does this mean?'

We are not told how old Joshua was when Moses came; looking at all the different dates I would put him in his thirties. By the time Moses comes on the scene, the chances are that Joshua had been working in slavery for a good fifteen years. I believe that in this time, Joshua learned to petition God—that with every brick he baked he asked in his heart 'what is this for?' that every time someone called his name he asked, 'where is it Lord?' I believe that Joshua learned to surround himself with the right people. In Numbers 13, we are told that Joshua and Caleb went to scope out the Promised Land (Canaan) together. Why are they together? The text tells us that leaders of the tribe were chosen. This must mean that these men were well respected, but I would suggest as well that they were friends, that they had been drawn together, that years before this happened they had formed a spirit-to-spirit friendship that fed into the heart of what God was doing. They had determined to be different. I believe Caleb watched the understudy and thought 'I want to be like that!'

Life is hard enough without surrounding yourself with people who are negative. Joshua had no choice in which walls he built, which materials he used, probably not even how many hours he worked, but he had a choice as to who he let speak into his spirit and from whom who he received counsel. I believe Joshua and Caleb spoke into each others' lives in difficult times. I imagine them talking each other up on bad days, reminding each other of the word of freedom that was over them. Only by doing this would they be able

---

[2]Henrietta Mears (ed.) *What is the Bible all about?* (Candle Books: Cumbria, 1999) p. 58

to stand strong in the desert while other people around them fell away. In Joshua 14: 12 Caleb comes to Joshua and says: *"Give me this hill country that the Lord has promised me that day, the Lord helping me, I will drive them out."* This is typical of Caleb's heart—he is a man who operates in a spirit that says, '*I'm here and I'm ready and I'm running,*' this spirit provokes Joshua's spirit as we then hear him in Joshua 18 challenging the rest of the Israelites '*how long will you wait before you begin to take possession of the land that the Lord, the God of your fathers has given you?"* (Verse 3). We need to surround ourselves with people who provoke a spirit response in us, these are not always people who will say things we want to hear, but they are people who will say things near to the heart of God.

Caleb was never going to be someone who led Joshua to a quiet life. You can almost imagine him going up to Joshua and saying '*I've got a plan*' and Joshua groaning inside thinking 'what now? Who does he want to fight now?' But Caleb was a provocation in the spirit to Joshua—an encouragement; he was also the right person. If Joshua had chosen anybody else the consequences could have been very grave.

When Joshua came out of Egypt, he left Egypt behind. The Israelites never left behind the mindset of captivity or of Egypt and, as a result, resorted back to Egyptian ways when they found themselves in difficult situations. Because they had never really left Egypt, they found it difficult to receive the provision of God in their circumstances. In Exodus 14 we see the Israelites say to Moses, *"was it because there were no graves in Egypt that you brought us into the desert to die?"* (Verse 12). The Israelites here reveal that their expectation for this journey is death—they have missed the point of their release. I wonder if in their hearts they held the cry of '*get us out of this place,*" whether they actually stopped to ask God, *"where are we going?"* God understands the cry of '*get me out*' because God understands the despair of our hearts but, when God takes us out of something, it is always because he wants to reveal more of his heart and more of his plan.

As a church we were given a prophetic word and part of this word said: *'I do not despise the despair of your heart, but know that I am the still small voice that pierces every situation. Let the place of desperation become the start of a journey to my mountain.³*

God recognises and understands our despair, he does not despise our pain and anguish but he meets us in our despair. We need to catch the still small voice of God in the noise of difficult circumstances; we need to allow our desperation to become intercession, because that intercession leads us on a journey to the heart of God.

Time after time the Israelites showed their heart for what they had come out of rather than their heart for what God was doing. For example:—Exodus 1: 3 *'in Egypt we sat round pots of meat and ate everything we wanted,'* Exodus 32: 4–5 tells the story of the golden calf and the Israelites looking back to the gods of the Egyptians—the ultimate slap in the face for God who was hand scribing a list of commandments onto stone for them at the time!

The Israelites were never free of their captivity because they never saw the freedom that God had given them. If they had seen what Joshua and Caleb had seen, they would have entered the Promised Land because that promise was for them as well. How much do we want what God has for us? Do we dare to pray—God open our eyes? When we truly catch something of the heart of God our spirit does not rest until we are running the way he has predestined for us. God's heart is to see all his children run into the freedom that he has. Freedom is not simply a thunderbolt of heaven that falls from the sky, but a daily choice, a daily confession that says: *'I am not looking back to things that didn't serve me well but I am looking forward into all God has promised me, I am looking with eyes of faith, that see it.'*

---

³Prophetic Word, Kings Community Church, Lancaster, England, 2008.

John 8: 36 states: *'Whoever the Son sets free shall be free indeed.'* We can know this and it can be a source of great frustration to us! I remember reading this scripture and thinking, *'but God, I'm not free.'* I am sure there were times Joshua looked at his circumstances and despaired. I am sure that there were times when he called out to God *'when will this end?'* But I believe Joshua learned to turn his despair to intercession, that this cry became a cry that pierced the throne room of God. We can do the same. Sometimes circumstances don't change, sometimes we don't feel free, but the truth of God stands in this—we are free.

It is time to step out of captivity and into freedom.

No going back
I am not looking back
Anymore
Because the locusts do not need
Anymore years,
They have had enough.

CHAPTER 2

A Journey of Choices

Joshua was a man who determined in his heart to make different choices. He saw the people around him consumed with bitterness and disappointment and chose something different for himself.

In Numbers 13:16 we see that Moses changed Joshua's name from Hoshea to Joshua. Hoshea means salvation and Joshua means the Lord's salvation.[4] Joshua could have rejected this name change or chosen to go by his other name but he doesn't, he embraces the gift that the man of God has given him. In embracing a new name, Joshua is also embracing a prophetic statement, not just for his lifetime but also for generations to come.

When we received salvation we received a new name, not a physical name change but a spiritual name change. We crossed over from a kingdom of darkness to a kingdom of light.

In Exodus 24 we see Moses and Joshua going up the mountain to receive the tablets of stone. Moses leaves Aaron and Hur in charge, and he and Joshua go up the mountain. I wonder why Joshua is there? At the start of Chapter 24, we see the command for Moses, Aaron, Nadab, and Abihu and seventy of the elders to come and worship at a distance, and they see a vision of God and eat and drink with him. The implication in the text is that Joshua is there as well and then in Verse 12 God says to Moses: *"Come up to me on the mountain and stay here, and I will give you the tablets of stone, with the law and commands I have written for*

---

[4]Henrietta Mears (ed.) *What is the Bible all about?* (Candle Books: Cumbria, 1999) p. 58

their instruction." So Moses and Joshua both go—but Moses alone enters the cloud and stays there forty days and forty nights.

I wonder why Joshua is there? I think when Moses moved, Joshua moved with him, that he was so used to serving Moses that he simply followed. He wanted to be where the revelation was. In the cloud, Moses receives detailed revelation from God on the ark, the tabernacle, the priests and the altars. In the meantime, the elders and Aaron finish their meal and start to panic. They go back down and are besieged by the people. They end up making a golden calf and encouraging the people to worship it. Joshua stays on the mountain. I wonder if he heard the elders leave the mountain and chose to stay where he was? I believe Joshua understood something of the fear of the Lord. I believe he spent those forty days worshipping, enjoying the provision of God, and asking God for his revelation.

I believe that on the mountain there was revelation for Joshua as well. I wonder if the whole situation with the golden calf would never have happened if the people had sought God? Or if the elders had stayed where they were? It can't have been easy for Joshua to stay on the mountain, with no provision, no one even to pray with. Joshua must have encountered something of God to stay. When we stand on the edge we find the provision of heaven, God does not simply leave us standing on the edge. I was in a cell group recently and we were praying. Someone shared a picture that they had received. It was of a person standing on a cliff edge getting ready to walk across and, just after the edge, was a pair of hands waiting to receive the first footstep. God doesn't take us to the edge to leave us there stranded. God takes us to the edge to display the miracle of his provision.

God is not restricted in his answer; he is abundant in his answer. When God led the Israelites out of Egypt, he took them to the edge. *"When Pharaoh let the people go, God did not lead them on the road through the Philistine country, though that was shorter. For God said, 'If they face war, they might change their minds and return to Egypt.' So God led the people around the desert road towards the Red Sea."* (Exodus 13: 17–18). God didn't take his people to the edge to prove a point, or to test them beyond their capabilities. God took his people to the edge for their own protection. He knew that they weren't ready to fight the battle that would have been there for them the other way. God took his people to the edge so they would witness the complete destruction of Pharaoh's army. God took them to the edge for them to see the waters piled up, for the assurance that he was with them on the journey. The edge was never intended to be a place of panic, it was meant to be a place of excitement. The edge was not meant to be a place of fear, but a place of anticipation. The edge was not meant to be a place of despair, but a place of rejoicing.

The Israelites missed the blessing of the edge because they were consumed by panic. My pastor often says, 'there's no panic in heaven, only plans!' Fear and panic are huge robbers of God's people. God's promise to his people is perfect peace. Isaiah 26: 3 says: *"You will keep in perfect peace him whose mind is steadfast, because he trusts in you."* It is an awesome thing to be able to stay calm in the midst of chaos. In Acts 12 we read about Peter's imprisonment and in Verse 6 we find him sleeping! When an angel appears to him and leads him out at first he thinks he is in a vision. It isn't until he is actually standing outside in the street that he realises this has happened. Peter's confidence is in God—there is a trust while asleep in prison that whatever happens, God is in control. Peter hadn't always been like this! Remember Peter walking on water? He started, then it must have dawned on him—'I'm walking on water'—and he began to sink.

In my life I have learned that the peace of God can supersede our circumstances. During my early twenties I went through a time of depression. To combat the awful blackness I felt I took medication, which meant I felt very numb instead. One of the things I was encouraged to do was to confess scripture over myself. I took great comfort in Psalm 131, which says:

> *My heart is not proud, O Lord, my eyes are not haughty; I do not concern myself with great matters or things too wonderful for me. But I have stilled and quietened my soul; like a weaned child with its mother, like a weaned child is my soul within me. O Rebecca[5] put your hope in the Lord, now and for evermore.*

I found that as I began to meditate on this I found stillness rather than numbness. Even now, I come back to that scripture again and again to remind myself that in God there is peace and there is stillness. My physical body and my head often try to tell me otherwise but, as I speak out that confession over my life, my body and my head have to take their proper place.

Sometimes in life we need to choose to stay on the mountain, to stay out of the fall-out of circumstance and rest in the revelation of God. Nehemiah was a man who knew opposition from people who didn't like the project God had given him. He remained focused on the task God had called him to even when his enemies did their best to interfere. Nehemiah 6: 2–4 says: *"Sanballat and Geshen sent me [Nehemiah] this message: 'Come, let us meet together in one of the villages on the plain of Ono.' But they were scheming to harm me; so I sent messages to them with this reply: 'I am carrying on a great project and cannot go down. Why should the work stop while I leave it and go down to you?' Four times they sent me the same message and each time I gave them the same answer."*

Nehemiah understood the importance of what God had called him to; he knew his position and his place. There is a security in knowing where you are meant to stand and with

---

[5]*My substitute—texts reads 'O Israel' (Psalm 131: 3)*

whom you are meant to stand. It is harder for your flesh to pull you away or for the enemy to distract you if you are standing in the right place doing the right thing. I wonder what would have happened if Aaron and the elders had stayed in the place where they had seen the vision, if they had lingered in the place of awe and worship before going back to the people? Joshua chose to stay on the mountain—this shows his heart to be where God is.

"I am too high to come down," is a powerful confession. It speaks to our mind, to our circumstances, and to those around us. When we confess that we are 'too high to come down' we are placing God in charge, putting him first. When we choose to put God first, our head and our circumstances have to line up with that because they are coming under the authority of God. Does that mean things change? No, not always, but we change, we are enabled to cope with whatever life throws at us and bring in the answers and order of heaven.

All of these things sound great, but what about the practical application? How do you make right choices when everybody around you is making wrong choices? For me there are three things we need to know: we need to know the heart of God, we need to know the word of God, and we need to understand who we journey with and where we are going.

Understanding the heart of God is key to realizing his plan for our lives. Too many Christians view God as a master obstacle race designer. A crafty course constructer who, just as you think you have finished the race, provides you with a cargo net to climb, or a strategist who waits for us to declare: 'I'm never going there/never doing that' to then announce—'I know just the man for the job'—and send you there to do that. Such an understanding of God completely misses the heart of God.

In life we are told to expect trouble. John 16: 33 reads: *'I have told you these things, so that you many have peace. In this world you will have trouble. But take heart! I have overcome the world.'* Jesus never promised us an easy ride, rather he promised us that things would be difficult, but the key is in the first part of the verse—peace. Life isn't easy, but in God there is ease in doing what he requires of us. The ease comes from understanding the victory—the war is already won. We fight battles every day, but the outcome of the war was decided at the cross. When we understand the heart of God, we understand that God wants to draw near to us, he wants to bless us, he wants to walk with us, and he wants to use us in extending his kingdom. We understand that we are not an afterthought, but a key part of kingdom tapestry. Understanding the heart of God knows God's heart is moved by our despair.

I recently attended the funeral of a friend. He was a Christian who had walked with God faithfully for many years and left behind a beautiful wife and a young son. They were a part of the much-loved church I grew up in and had maintained links with over the years.

Walking into the funeral service was like walking back in time twenty years—everybody was there. People I hadn't seen for years, who remembered me as a little girl, my own childhood friends with husbands and babies of their own, former Sunday school teachers, crèche workers, and friends. All with one thing in common—Jesus and the testimony of how he had walked with us and what he had done across twenty years. One of the deacons shared and talked about how Andrew would be in heaven, playing rugby with Brian, having coffee with Tony, and eating cake with Rose (all friends who had passed away some years before). And we all half-laughed and half-cried together because that is the heart of the kingdom of God. It looks beyond, from an eternal perspective. Were we sad? Of course we were, and my heart broke for Julie and her son Christopher because their loss was greatest. But that day was a day of incredible testimony when heaven touched earth. Awesome. All of us were reduced to tears when Andrew's father spoke and, through his tears, said with great determination: "I'm celebrating because I know where Andrew is." This reminds me of Jesus dying on the cross when he said with a shout of triumph. *"It is finished."* (John 19: 30). That cry was no cry of despair but a cry that declared death had no more power.

God is not hard to our suffering. He does not despise our despair but he longs for us to understand his heart because, in his heart, we grasp the 'it is finished.' The heart of God sees the eternal perspective. Paul writes: *"Therefore we do not lose heart. Though outwardly we are wasting away, yet inwardly we are being renewed day by day. For our light and momentary troubles are achieving for us an eternal glory that far outweighs them all. So we fix our eyes not on what is seen, but on what is unseen. For what is seen is temporary, but what is unseen is eternal."* (2 Corinthians 4: 16–18). From an earthly perspective, Paul's troubles weren't light! This was a man who was often persecuted, shipwrecked and in prison, who knew physical hardship and spiritual grief but he had seen something more. Paul was so caught up with what he had seen in God that his troubles shrank to the position of being light and momentary—they took their right position in the order of heaven. Were they really light and momentary? I suspect not, but they became a small inconvenience rather than an insurmountable problem. When Paul was bitten by a snake, he shook it off (Acts 28:3–6), when he was shipwrecked, he healed the sick (Acts 28: 7–9), when he was under house arrest, he preached the gospel (Acts 28: 30–31). He lived with his eyes on heaven and so earth moved. It gave up its position to be touched by the miracle power of heaven. In understanding the heart of God, we need to ask what it means to live in a place of coming out of a shipwreck, shaking of the vipers and preaching the word.

As well as knowing God's heart, we need to be a people that know God's word. Joshua was able to make the right choices because he knew the word of God. We need to be a people who know and apply the written word of God and the prophetic word of God to our lives. Joshua knew the word of God over the Israelites, he was a descendant of Joseph and Joseph had declared on his deathbed: *"I am about to die. But God will surely come to your aid and take you up out of this land to the land he promised on oath to Abraham, Isaac and Jacob."* And Joseph made the sons of Israel swear an oath and said, *"God will surely come to your aid, and then you must carry my bones up from this place."* (Genesis 50: 25). Joshua knew that Joseph had seen what God was going to do. I believe Joshua knew and treasured the word God had given Abraham. *"I will surely bless you and make your descendants as numerous as the stars in the sky and as the sand on the seashore. Your descendants will take possession of the cities of their enemies, and through your offspring, all nations on earth will be blessed because you have obeyed me."* (Genesis 22: 17–18). Joshua understood the word of God in his situation, he understood the promise, and he understood the instruction. Because Joshua understood the promise and the instruction, he was able to stand in the integrity of the decisions he made—a statement that said 'we will get there and we will be blessed but we must stick to what is right.' Because Joshua knew the word, he was able to stand when everybody else berated Moses, saying: *"Why did you bring us up out of Egypt to make us and our children and livestock die of thirst?"* (Exodus 17: 3b). I can almost imagine Joshua's frustration as he looks at his friends and family and thinks to himself 'you don't get it—that's not part of God's plan.' If we want to experience the ease of God in difficult circumstances, we need to understand the word of God into our situations and be prepared to speak it in, even when things don't look great.

I was out driving a couple of years ago with my friend who is sometimes a bit of a pessimist. We reached a very busy junction and she sighed and said, "They'll never let us out." I laughed and responded, "Yes, they will," and then said casually, "we need to get out God." Sure enough, the next car stopped and flashed its lights at us, and we pulled out and drove away. My friend was flabbergasted and I just laughed.

I expect God to do me good. Driving to my friend's funeral I needed a parking space and there was a small car park close to the church. I told my grandma of my intention to park there, she responded, "You won't get a space there." I replied, "God will give me a parking space." Sure enough, when I arrived there was a space there for me, the last one in the car park. God delights in the faith of his people. These are just small things, but people see, people are watching. If we want to see God do miracles, we need to live in the expectancy that he will.

Life is a journey of choices; we need to be careful whom we journey with, because our journey companions can affect our destination. Joshua was part of a people who were journeying together, he had no choice in that, but he found a spirit-to-spirit companion. Exodus 12:37 tells us that six hundred thousand men, plus women and children, left Egypt—in all of this Joshua had found the one man who shared his heart, Caleb. Joshua's choice of Caleb as a friend enabled him and encouraged him on his journey to the Promised Land. We need to know with whom we are walking. It would have been easy for Joshua to have been robbed of his appointment by everybody else's disappointment, but he refused to give up on the word of God. Joshua positioned himself instead by the man of God—Moses. He chose to live in the place of the understudy and to know more about what it meant to draw near to God. Joshua knew that Moses had something—the Bible tells us that the Lord knew Moses face to face (Deuteronomy 34: 10) and Joshua chose to walk after that.

We need to choose to be with people who are living in the appointment of God. We need to choose to be people who encourage others into the appointment of God. We need to be in churches that are moving in the anointing and the power of God. Churches that are hungry for the heart of God, which are preaching the word of God. Dead wood is a dangerous place to be because it doesn't contribute to a fire that inspires and spreads. You can't live in dead wood unless you have a clear word from God—otherwise, you will lose what you have.

Every choice has an outcome. I want the outcome of every choice I make to be that the kingdom of God extends—otherwise, I am making the wrong choices.

CHAPTER 3

Commander in Chief

Joshua was a man of incredible authority; he saw what Moses had and drew on Moses' testimony. Joshua knew that one day he would take on the mantle of leadership and he stood with Moses and gleaned everything he could before that time approached. We need to know who we are understudying. We need to be aware of who we are allowing to speak to our spirits.

The church in Galatia became confused when they stopped listening to the teaching of their apostle and started listening to other people (who had the wrong idea) instead. Paul challenged the Galatians in Galatians 5: 7 saying, *"You were running a good race, who cut in on you and kept you from obeying the truth?"* Paul knew the security of accountability and following the truth. Paul knew the dangers of listening and standing under wrong authority. After all, he had zealously stood under the wrong authority for years persecuting God's people.

It would have been very easy for Joshua to keep well away from Moses. I'm sure there were other men who fancied themselves as leaders, and I'm sure there was plenty of muttering. I'm sure that there was also plenty of jealousy directed at Joshua.

In Exodus 17: 8–16 we see Moses and Joshua battling the Amalekites. Joshua's role in this battle was Commander in Chief—he is on the battlefield with the troops. Moses is the intercessor, and he stands on the top of the hill with his hands held high. While Moses hands are up, the Israelites are winning; when he lowers his hands they lose. Eventually, when Moses is exhausted, Aaron and Hur hold his hands up for him, and so Joshua overcomes and the Israelites win the battle.

In this passage, we see Joshua beginning to take up the mantle of leadership, we see between the two men and understanding of role. Moses—the man who sees God face-to-face and speaks with him—is the intercessor. He stands in the gap between heaven and earth. He stands with faithful men who hold the anointing with him when he can't physically manage anymore. Joshua is the army commander, the strategist; the one who stands in the purposes of God to enable the plan of God.

In Exodus 17: 9 we see the trust between Moses and Joshua as Moses turns to Joshua and says: *"Choose some of our men and go out to fight the Amalekites. Tomorrow I will stand on top of the hill with the staff of God in my hands."* Notice that Moses is not only telling Joshua to choose, he is not going into battle with him or providing him with a plan. I believe there was an unsaid expectation there from Moses *"seek God for who you should take and what the plan is."* There is also recognition from Moses that Joshua hears God and is capable of leading the people, he can walk in confidence away from the battle because the anointing rests heavy over Joshua. I wonder what Joshua felt when Moses walked away? You can almost imagine Joshua thinking to himself 'great, he's going up the mountain and I'm on my own.' I imagine Joshua going back to his tent and praying 'who do I take, how do I do this?' Joshua had to put aside how he felt in order to get ready for the battle, he had to choose into the role God had prepared for him rather than run after Moses. On the morning of the battle Joshua arrives ready. Exodus 17:10 tells us that, *"Joshua fought the Amalekites as Moses had ordered, and Moses, Aaron, and Hur went to the top of the hill."* I wonder how Joshua felt as he saw the three elders walking away from him up the hill? I believe in taking on the leadership of the army that day he found fresh anointing in the mantle of leadership over him.

Sometimes our strategies for winning battles aren't the same as God's. I wonder if Joshua thought 'if it was me, I'd stand Moses at the front of the army and have him raise his staff high and smite them all with a thunderbolt. I wouldn't be sending him up a hill, away from the army and tell him to put his hands in the air.' Thank goodness we do not need to tell God how to win the battle or provide him with the answers. Often God has a different way.

In 2 Kings 5 the commander of the army of the king of Aram (Naaman) comes to see the prophet Elisha wanting to be healed of leprosy. Elisha tells him to bathe in the Jordan River seven times and he will be healed. Naaman is not very impressed and responds saying *"I thought that he would surely come out to me and stand and call on the name of the Lord his God, wave his hand over the spot and cure me of my leprosy. Are not Abana and Pharpar, the rivers of Damascus better than any of the rivers of Israel? Couldn't I wash in them and be cleansed?"* Naaman had missed the point—God isn't like a magic wand, he doesn't always grant us what we ask for. Naaman wanted some kind of grand miracle—some big event that he felt reflected his splendour. God chose instead to humble by making him wash seven times in a dirty river. I wonder how his attitude changed each time. I bet the first time he was furious, the second time he would still be cross, the third time, slightly annoyed, the fourth and fifth times resigned, the sixth time, maybe expectant, the seventh time completely humbled. All his life people had only told him what he wanted to hear and pandered to his wishes and, now, the one man who refused to do so had done something nobody else could. In losing his pride Naaman lost the idol he had become to himself and found instead the awe of living in a miracle. We see in 2 Kings 5: 15 Naaman exclaiming *"I get it, it's all about God. Who is this God? What can I give you?"*[6]

We cannot dictate our answers to God. In the provision of a miracle, there are always things God wants us to learn and

[6]My paraphrase: 2 Kings 5:15

take away. For Joshua there was victory in the battle, and Joshua saw again the battle was the Lord's—God was the one fighting. The place of the army, the place of the intercessor, the place of friendship, of discipleship, was the place of obedience. The only thing Joshua needed to do was be in the right place and fight the battle; the only thing Moses needed to do was hold up his hands; the only thing Aaron and Hur needed to do was make sure he could.

Sometimes we make the mistake of thinking God needs our assistance to fulfill his promises, or we panic because God seems to be tarrying in his response. Look at Sarah and Hagar—the promise of God was unaffected. Sarah gave birth to her own son, Isaac, but the effect of Sarah's meddling can be seen even today in the conflict between the Arabs (descended from Ishmael) and the Israelites (descended from Isaac). Habakkuk writes about the revelation of God, recording God's response *"The Lord replied: 'Write down the revelation and make it plain on tablets that a herald may run with it. For the revelation awaits an appointed time; it speaks of the end and will not prove false. Though it linger, wait for it; it will certainly come and not delay.'"*[7]

Joshua knew what it meant to live in the place of inhabiting the revelation of God, seeking the appointed time, and moving in obedience.

Joshua was a man who saw great victory. We see that in this battle (the first battle), that *"Joshua overcame the Amalekite army with the sword."* (Exodus 17:13). This was to be the start of a series of battles that Joshua would fight over many years. Joshua Chapter 12 gives a list of defeated kings and causes us to understand the magnitude of the battles Joshua fought. Joshua was an overcomer; throughout his journey he had learned to lean into God and as a result saw God do amazing things.

I believe Joshua was a good fighter, a good strategist, but most importantly, he understood that the victory was God's.

---

[7]Habakkuk 2: 2–3

In Joshua 23 we read Joshua's farewell to the leaders. Verse 3 reads, *"You yourselves [Israel's leaders] have seen everything the Lord your God has done to all these nations for your sake; it was the Lord your God who fought for you."* Joshua understood that the plan, the victory and the purpose belonged to God; his place was simply the place of obedience. His confession could have been a very different one, he could have said: 'You've seen what God has done and half the time still complained and grumbled about it, you gave me a hard time when I was right, you gave me a hard time when I was wrong, and still God didn't smite you, when will you understand God has a plan?' Joshua operates in grace— he knows that only his choices separate him from the rest of the leaders.

We can be in the plans of God, see the miracles of God but miss the victory of God in our lives. There was no need for anyone in the wilderness to die. In Exodus fifteen Moses sings a prophetic song declaring, *"You will bring them [The Israelites] in and plant them on the mountain of your inheritance"* (Exodus 15:17). The choices the people made cost them the joy of seeing the Promised Land. A lot of the choices the Israelites made were based on things they perceived they didn't have—water, food, a strong enough army, a good leader—they missed the point. God was the provider. In God we have all the resources that we need, all the answers for whatever things we face. We miss the point sometimes when we try to solve our problems our way, when we look for answers that seem elusive; when in giving God our yes we release the answer of heaven.

I remember, some years ago now, talking with a friend. We were both facing difficult situations and they were dragging us down. We used to say to one another "I am an overcomer, I chose to overcome." Sometimes, I think we wanted to slap the other person! But it worked—it reminded our spirits of who we were. We are so good sometimes at reminding ourselves of who we're not—why do the enemy's job for him?

I have never forgotten that confession. I think we said it to each other enough times! If we want to live in the victory of heaven, we need to remind ourselves that that is our inheritance. Sometimes we don't feel like overcomers, we don't see the victory, and there aren't answers. God is still God. God brings his reality into our situations so heaven's answers transform earth's perspective.

What does it mean to live life as an overcomer? Can I suggest three things? When we live as an overcomer, we live in the confidence of the Word of God, the character of God, and the answers of heaven. This means that we feed ourselves daily on the Word of God – we carve time out of our lives to hear and understand the promises of God. *"The word of God is the sword of the Spirit"* (Ephesians 6: 17), it is a key weapon with which we demolish the strongholds of the enemy, it shields our thinking from wrong ideals, it is our benchmark, our plumb line against which we test thoughts and ideas. Knowing the character of God means we understand something of the awesomeness of his majesty, we understand the fear of the lord. Knowing the character of God means drawing near to him, approaching him as a father, petitioning him as a king. James 4:8 says *"Draw near to God and he will draw near to you."* God desires a people who draw near to him, in drawing near to him our heads are raised over our circumstances, over our situations, and we see from God's perspective. God is an overcomer—death could not hold him! In drawing near to him we catch hold of a heart that sings above death.

When we trust in the answers of heaven, that means that whatever happens we are not shaken—that we know God will have his way, he will work out his purposes. Trusting in the answers of heaven is a release when things happen that we don't understand.

As we overcome we need to make sure God gets the glory. After the battle we see the Lord saying to Moses *"Write this on a scroll as something to be remembered and make sure that Joshua hears it, because I will completely blot out the memory of Amalek from under heaven."* (Exodus 17: 14). I love the imperative instruction—make sure Joshua hears it! I can just imagine God saying to Moses, *"He needs to know that this was important, that I'll always fight for him, that I'm setting a standard, that when he lifts his hands towards me I will win the victory!"* Joshua needed to know that this victory was important; this victory provided the blueprint for other battles, an encouragement when he was feeling low and courage when he was feeling weak. God knows our tendency to forget, that's why he gives us tangible things to remember them by—the Old Testament is full of alters, for example, in Genesis 8: 20 Noah built an altar to thank God for his deliverance from the flood, in Genesis 13: 18 Abram built an altar to God at Hebron just after God had given him a promise. God wants a people who remember—a people who remember are a secure people, a confident people. Upon an altar is a sacrifice, it is burnt until it is unrecognisable—it is symbolic first of Jesus, Isaiah writes *"... there were many who were appalled at him—his appearance was so disfig-ured beyond that of any man and his form marred beyond human likeness."* (Isaiah 52: 14), but out of that sacrifice came resurrection life.

Altars are also symbolic of our circumstance, they sig-nify an end. When Noah built his altar where did he get the wood? I have a feeling he took the wood from the ark and used the first portion of it to build an altar, that altar went up as a declaration that the old order had ended and the world was beginning again. It was starting with praise. Noah's al-tar moved God's heart and God declared *"Never again will I curse the ground because of man"* (Genesis 8: 21). Ev-ery time Noah looked at that altar he would remember both the deliverance of God and the promise of God. Every time Joshua looked at the scroll he would remember both the promise of God and the deliverance of God.

The altar principle is something we can employ in our own lives—do we go and buy some wood from B and Q, some meat from Sainsbury's and have a bonfire—no! But we establish things in our hearts that act as a reminder of the faithfulness of God.

When I was twenty-two, I was off work with an eating disorder and feeling rubbish. I had received prayer, I knew the promises of God, but somehow it all seemed very distant from me. It had been a very challenging weekend and God had already spoken into my life on the Saturday. I went to church that Sunday wondering what was going to happen. I went forward for prayer, and I knew God had done something. I felt I was healed. To test my healing I went out and ate a three-course lunch. By all rights I should have been very sick, but I wasn't. God did it! That meal became my altar, my benchmark, my never again. That day it was prophesied that there was no going back—this was the end.

Since that day I have never had a day off because of my eating disorder. Have I struggled? There have been times when it has been difficult, but I am reminded of that altar because it reminds me that there is no going back.

When Noah built his altar it was a declaration, his sailing days were over! He didn't need the ark anymore, he wasn't going to keep it moored somewhere just in case! When God called Elisha, Elisha used the wood from his plough to make a fire and then sacrificed the oxen. He was making a declaration, 'I'm going this way now.' He destroyed his choice, he didn't have the option to go back and be a farmer because he had destroyed the tools of his trade.

Joshua was a man who understood the altar principle. When the Israelites crossed the Jordan, they took with them twelve stones—stones that would remain in place after the water had gone back. Those stones signified as a reminder that God had given them this land and saved them from captivity. (Joshua 4).

Joshua's last act was to set up an altar (Joshua 24: 25–27)—a stone near the holy place of God that would serve to remind the people of their decision to follow God. Am I advocating that we leave behind us a trail of stones? Somehow

I don't think that would make us very popular, but we need to remember, tangibly, the goodness of God. We were encouraged at church to keep a record of three things we were grateful to God for each day. When we live in a spirit of gratitude we see more clearly, our eyes become more fixed on that which God has given us and wants to give us, rather than on things we don't have.

In Exodus 17, Moses names the altar, he calls it 'The Lord is my Banner.' I wonder if every time Moses looked at the altar he laughed as he remembered holding his hands up for hours and hours! Sometimes in the Bible altars are given names—often where altars are named this is of prophetic significance. In Genesis 22:14 just after God had provided a ram in place of Isaac, Abraham names the altar 'The Lord Will Provide'—a prophetic declaration of the sacrifice of Jesus. What do we name the altars in our lives? What do we declare over our circumstances? What is the prophetic significance of the altars that we build?

Let us not confuse altars with idols. Idols are things that put themselves as more important than God. Idols need to become altars; the place of idolatry is a place where we give something more importance than God. The place of sacrifice—of being at the altar—is where we acknowledge the sovereignty of God. In Judges 6, the first thing God called Gideon to do was to transform a place of idolatry into a place of sacrifice, into an altar. This was not a call the mighty warrior relished and he chose to change it round at night time. For Gideon that act became his altar, in trashing the altar of Baal and building an altar to God he was giving his and his families lives over to God. If we want to see the miracle power of God at work, the idols in our lives must be replaced with altars.

God is a jealous God, he will not share his glory with another. He will not share his place with anything else. I have read the story in Exodus 17 but never really appreciated the magnitude of it before. What must it have felt like for Joshua to watch Moses, Aaron, and Hur climb the mountain, away from the battle, to explain their departure to the troops, to lead the Israelites into battle with a plan, knowing the plan rested on Moses hands staying in the air?

I think Joshua never forgot that day—that something broke in him when Moses lifted his staff in the air, and he knew in his spirit that this was it. A mantle of leadership was passed to Joshua that day. When Moses left to climb that mountain he recognized something of the Spirit of God in Joshua. Part of me wonders if the cry of *'make sure Joshua hears it'* was a cry from his own testimony of *'make sure Joshua remembers God goes first.'* Moses anger cost him the fulfillment of his vision. He would see at a distance something that he could have seen up close. Joshua saw differently, he was buried in the land of his inheritance (Joshua 24:30); I believe he caught something that day. The name of the altar 'God is My Banner' was a cry from a man who'd got it wrong, to the next in line to carry the mantle, a cry of *'God sees, God hears, God covers you, God gives you the grace to cope with these people, God is your sustenance, your source, your direction, your provision.'* As Joshua looked at that altar he realised, possibly for the first time, his destiny. As he took that scroll from Moses he chose to carry that experience close to his heart.

Altars do not travel with us, they are points in a journey, sometimes we return to them, and sometimes we never see them again. They are not a place of pilgrimage. At every altar we leave something of ourselves. In the Old Testament when they sacrificed an animal, they would sacrifice something that they would humanly want, need, or could make profit from. Once the animal was sacrificed that was it, it was dead. The things we sacrifice on the altars of our journey are meant to stay on the altar, not come with us. We are too good sometimes at making travelling idols of items required for sacrifice.

CHAPTER 4

A Man Who Stood
on the Mountain

Come with me on a journey. We have reached Mt Sinai and are camped in front of the mountain. The air is thick with expectation as people wait to see what will happen, children cry and laugh, and the atmosphere is fractious with anticipation. Moses seemed distracted somehow as he looked away into the distance, at something we can't see. Then a rumble of thunder, a growl so deep it reached into the core of our hearts, but no rain, no lightening, just the sound and Moses strode to the foot of the mountain. It was like time stood still and we waited, caught in the moment. When he came back and raised his staff into the air, a ripple of silence, more than six thousand strong spread through our company, and the elders walked to the front and stood before the man of God and then the whisper reached us, spread backwards like the wind,

"Says the Lord, I carried you, now keep my covenant, be my treasured possession, my kingdom of priests, my holy nation." And like a tidal wave we knelt, a word came from the very heart of the people, over and over, 'yes, yes, yes.' Moses surveyed us, his eyes piercing every heart, you could cut the air with a sword, as silence fell heavy, like a blanket, like the hand of God and then the cloud descended and we didn't dare speak. We were told not to climb the mountain or we would surely die, but to wait, wait for the single blast of a ram's horn.

And so we watched the mountain in awe and horror and smoke billowed and fire ringed the tip, as the very earth trembled and thunder and lightning split the sky, and as the rain kept falling and falling it began to seem like a picture far away.

And then he appeared again and beckoned the elders and spoke to us and the fire on the mountain burned brighter than before, flames of gold and orange—all consuming but never burning. And we heard the words of the covenant and we responded, "We will obey," and we felt it, a fearful confession, a truthful confession, a heartfelt confession, we meant it—or at least we thought we did.

And then the elders followed him without question, the younger ones bounding ahead in their anticipation, and the older ones leaning heavily on their staffs. They disappeared up the mountain, leaving us to stare at the fire and smoke and wonder. And silence. No ram's horn. No trumpet. No thunder. No lightning. No leaders.

And then the whispers started, whispers like lasso's that ran the length of the camp and back and no one came. Days. Nights. Weeks.

And then a steady trickle of elders like raindrops down the mountain. They seemed almost drunk, unable to describe what they had seen, a world apart, an experience away and then last of all Aaron and Hur, two old men came down the mountain. Leaning heavily on their staffs, traces of glory etched on their lined faces, marred with the agony of waiting. They hadn't seen Moses, they hadn't seen Joshua, and they feared them dead.

I don't think Aaron appreciated the effect of his words that threw the camp into panic, 'dead,' the women screamed, 'dead,' the children copied, crying, 'dead,' the men despaired, and the humming grew like angry bees. "We are here to die," the people wailed in despair, "God has brought us here to destroy us," and then they rounded on Aaron, "do something," they demanded, and Aaron, desperate to appease them, to soothe them, to prevent chaos, collected gold—all their earrings—and melted them down. He crafted a beautiful golden calf, fashioning it with careful touches, and the people stood by and watched, children touched it in wonder, a brooding calm seemed restored. "It is a god," the people murmured. Aaron tried at first to refute them, but they became angry and said among themselves: "This is the god that brought us out of Egypt." And the confession grew like a bush fire until it had taken over the camp. The people laughed and whooped with joy, prostrating themselves before the idol as Aaron looked on in horror, " A festival," Aaron announced, a remedy. "We will have a festival to the Lord tomorrow." So the morning dawned and Aaron led us in sacrifice, but there was no awe only giddiness as the people laughed and danced and mimicked the parties they had once seen, and the peace soon gave way to revelry, madness, drunkenness, lust, and Aaron began to wonder 'what have I done?'

A world away, Moses and Joshua walked down the mountain, slowly, silently, thinking. Still in a place of revelation. And then they heard the noise, great shouts and screams as if a battle was raging below and Joshua looked at Moses, troubled. "The camp is at war," he said.

"That is no war," said Moses, gazing down to the foot of the mountain. And he strode with a force, hurling his words behind him, "That is no war, no victory or defeat, that is the sound of singing," and he looked at the scenes before him and with a mighty roar threw the stones in his hand into the camp. The tablets, the very word of God, inscribed by his hand, shattered into pieces and caused lines to run the length of where they lay. And his eyes sought out Aaron with a fire that caused people to look away, and he whispered to his brother, "What did you do to these people to lead them into this great sin?" And Aaron had no answer and watched as Moses burnt the idol, ground it to powder, and he was the first to drink the gold. And then the Levites rallied to Moses side and roamed the camp, killing thosewhot had not come to Moses' side, and the desert ran red with blood, staining every tent, every sword, every tribe and Moses, the man of God, went to stand in the gap for his people once again.

"If you will not forgive them," he cried in passion, "then do not forgive me, for I am one of them." And God saw the heart of his servant and said, "Go, lead my people, know that *my angel goes before you, but know also that I am just." And comforted, Moses left. God, the God of justice, struck the people with a plague in punishment for the calf before he led them on again.*

And Moses spoke to God, face to face, a friendship deep and strong, and Joshua—Joshua worshipped.

LEARNING FROM THE MAN ON THE MOUNTAIN

1.   Joshua lived in the place of promise.

The more I look at the life of Joshua, the more I am staggered by the magnitude of his choices. It is a truly awesome thing to be able to stand against everybody else in total security, knowing that you are doing the right thing.

At the start of this stage in the Israelites journey, they are given a powerful promise, they have just arrived at Mt Sinai, and God calls Moses from the mountain with a word,

> *"You yourselves have seen what I did to Egypt and how I carried you on eagle's wings and brought you to myself. Now if you obey me fully and keep my covenant, then out of all nations you will be my treasured possession, although the whole earth is mine, you will be for me a kingdom of priests and a holy nation"*
>
> *Exodus 19: 4–6*

I believe Joshua caught hold of this word. He knew that when God gave a promise it was for a reason. The first part of the promise was a warning, *'remember what I did to Egypt?'* The Israelites saw Pharaohs entire army drown before their eyes, they saw the Egyptians struck by plague after plague. They knew just how severe the hand of God could be. God is a God of justice—that means he is wholly just. God's justice isn't just for our enemies, but for our own lives as well. When we make the decision to follow Jesus we are entering into a whole new way of living, a whole new regime. The old systems don't apply anymore, you can't bring old values and old ways of doing things and slot them into a new way of life; God's kingdom doesn't work like that. Paul writes in 1 Corinthians *"The body that is sown is perishable, it is raised imperishable, it is sown in dishonour, it is raised in glory; it is sown in weakness, it is raised in power; it is sown a natural body, it is raised a spiritual body."* (1 Corinthians 15: 42–44). What is Paul saying here? Paul is reminding the Corinthians that they are a spiritual people, that actually what they live in is the reality of God's miraculous power, the knowledge that the Holy Spirit is longing to pour out his power, the promise of strength to endure. Joshua had caught something that other people missed. When Joshua received the word from Mt Sinai, he recognized a change again a shift in the Spirit. Joshua had left behind captivity, shaken the dust off his sandals when he walked out of Egypt, now, having heard the promise, he began to step into this next promise. He walked as part of a kingdom of priests, a holy nation (Exodus: 19:5–6). He understood that the journey wasn't finished, it was only just beginning.

I believe that for a lot of the Israelites when they left Egypt, they thought the journey was over—that was it. They expected maybe six months or a year until they got to their new home. They planned out their lives in their minds—what they would plant, how they would live, etc. There was almost arrogance in knowing *'Yes, we are God's favoured nation,'* but no inward acceptance of that—no thought process that said *'If we are a holy nation, what does this mean?'*

We cannot be a people who live just in the place of fulfilled promise; we need to be living in the revelation of the unfulfilled promises over our lives. I imagine Joshua going to God and saying, *'What does it mean to be your treasured possession? What does it mean to be a holy nation?'* Sometimes we don't understand the words over our lives. Is that because we are not seeking the revelation of things that God has imparted to us? God rarely gives us the whole plan; sometimes we get an overview, sometimes the first chapter, sometimes only the first line! The answers will never be completely ours this side of heaven—that is not meant to be a source of frustration, but a source of hope.

Living in a place of fulfilled promise says to God *'Because you did this, you can do that,'* living in a place of unfulfilled promise asks the question *'What does it mean to be me, here, at this time—how do I fulfill your word over my life?'*

2.   *Joshua was part of the initial 'yes'*

In Exodus 19:8 we see the initial response of the elders (and I suspect Joshua was in this). The elder's say to Moses, *'We will do everything the Lord has said.'* I imagine an almost instantaneous response that said, *'Wonderful, God's treasured possession!'* I wonder if they had clocked the prerequisite, the obedience to the covenant and to God himself. Yes was the right response, but it was given without a right understanding. Saying yes to God is a serious thing—God wants a committed people and not a fickle people.

I was in church a couple of months back and we were singing a new setting of a very famous song. Not knowing the tune, I fumbled my way through and didn't really think about what I was singing. Later on as I remembered this, some of the verses really challenged me, and I was convicted about what I had sung,

> Take my silver and my gold
> Not a mite would I withhold,
> Take my intellect and use,
> Every power as Thou shall choose,
>
> Take my will and make it Thine,
> It shall be no longer mine,
> Take my heart, it is Thine own,
> It shall be Thy royal throne.[8]

---

[8]"Take My Life and Let It Be" is a hymn by Frances Ridley Havegal (1836–79)

I had to really go back over my life and say honestly—am I tithing properly and giving generously. If God told me he wanted all my money could I do it? Am I prepared to let God use my intellect, to be diligent in writing the books I believe he has laid on my heart, to do any courses he would have me do? (I have to admit, my heart plummeted at the thought of being a student again!) Am I prepared to go where you want me to go? If you said move, could I do it? (But I really don't want to move. I am happy where I am!) Are you really the first in my heart? (Ouch!)

It is very easy to be critical of the Israelites—how quick they were to say yes and how fast to turn away. But when I looked at myself that Sunday, I realize that actually I am not so different. My heart's desire is to please God; my mouth is quick to declare it, but sometimes my flesh it a little slow in keeping pace. Joshua was a man whose yes was yes. James 5 talks about the importance of our yes being yes, *"Above all my brothers, do not swear—not by heaven or by earth or by anything else. Let your "yes" be yes, and your "no," no, or you will be condemned"* (James 5:12). God is looking for a people whose yes, means yes. Does that mean we always get it right? No, of course not. God understands we are not perfect, but God demands honesty.

I remember once being challenged in a student meeting about singing the worship songs. The worship leader encouraged us to read the words before we sang them and then sing them or not sing them, but not half sing—i.e., not lie before God. This was something that always stayed with me.

Sometimes we can sing songs in faith or as a declaration over our circumstances. There is a powerful worship song that declares *'I will be still and know you are God.'*[9] I have sung that song when I have been in turmoil, but I have sung it as a cry, a command to my flesh to respond to the promises

[9]"Still" Words and Music by Reuben Morgan, Hillsongs Church, Australia. 2002

of God, to be still in the panic. I believe God responds to that 'yes' cry.

We need to be a people who live out our response to God—a people who after we have given our yes, work out the understanding of that. When Joshua gave his yes, I believe he went back to God with his yes and said, 'What does this mean?' For Joshua that yes meant he stayed on the mountain when everybody else came down.

In 2005–2006 I worked as a music teacher in a school an hour away from where I lived. I was struggling with the commute every day and wanted a change. I applied for different jobs, but nothing happened. I went for an interview and withdrew halfway through because I knew it wasn't right. It was fast approaching the last day for resigning and there was nothing. It looked like I was staying where I was. In tears I drove to work, praying in my car, *'God I don't want to stay another year, but if that's what you want me to do, I will stay.'* On the last possible day I could resign I was offered an interview at a school ten minutes down the road from where I lived. I got the job and handed in my resignation. Everything fit exactly together and then, during my time at my new school, they released me into other things.

That day, I learned a powerful lesson about our yes to God. When we place ourselves in total submission, he releases us into his perfect plan. Joshua walked out his yes to God by staying on the mountain—the right position. The other elders were relying on an emotional response; their yes had been a heat of the moment, a good intentioned, right answer with no depth. Emotional responses will only lead us as far as the next experience, if we want to be a people of depth we need to go back and ask God again and again and again what it means to give him our yes.

3. *Joshua went through a time of consecration*

God is never just about the initial response, God is a God of strategy, timing, and planning. The instructions in Exodus

19: 10–11 are for the people to wash their clothes, to conse-crate themselves, and be ready for the third day. Let us for a moment consider the symbolism of the third day. When Jesus died on the cross there was the crucifixion and then, on the third day, the resurrection.[10]

This time of consecration was meant to be a time of ac-ceptance of the word God had given. A time when the Isra-elites considered what God had done, that as they washed their clothes they remembered God's redemption of them from slavery, that as they prepared to hear the voice of God, they asked God what it meant to be his holy nation. I imagine Joshua, washing his clothes and asking God, *'Prepare me, cleanse me on the inside, and make me ready.'* To consecrate something is to dedicate it to the service of God. I wonder how many of the Israelites had really engaged with the pro-cess of consecration.

As a kingdom people, we are a people consecrated to God. We live in the world, but we are not of the world. Our walk with God starts with our confession, but it continues with our consecration. Too many Christians stop at the confession and miss out on the blessings of consecration. Consecration costs you. It is not an easy thing. God calls us to consecrate the big things and the little things. I remember as a teenager, declaring just before a women's meeting that I really felt God had called me to be a back person, and that I was happy with that, and that was right. The next second I felt a tap on my shoulder and a summons from the worship leader – *"Becki, we need another singer, will you come and join the worship team tonight?."* I think my jaw hit the floor as those around me laughed. I protested—loudly, but in the end I gave in to the gentle but insentience of the very gracious woman who was leading that night. I knew in that moment that my days of being a back person were over and I gave that to God. God had answered my agenda with his plan and that meeting became my consecration. In the following years I went on to

_____
[10]See John's Gospel: 19–20

lead worship in youth services at different churches, I gave over my heart to hide at the back!

Once, in moving to a new house, God convicted me about some of the books on my shelf. I sorted through them on the premise that if I couldn't lend them to my youth group, they would be binned. I hate throwing away books, but I knew that a couple of them needed to be binned. I look at both the books and the singing, and I am so blessed that these areas of my life are consecrated to God. It is an awesome privilege to stand and lead God's people in worship, my life is better without those books because my mind is filled with better things. Paul writes *"But whatever was to my profit I now consider loss for the sake of Christ. What is more I consider everything a loss compared to the surpassing greatness of knowing Christ Jesus my Lord, for whose sake I have lost all things. I consider them rubbish, that I may gain Christ and be found in him."* (Philippians 3: 7–9)

When I think that consecration is difficult, when the cost of what I am laying down seems too much, I remind myself that Jesus became sin—that which was unholy in order that I can be holy.

4.   The intention was that eventually the people would come up the mountain

In Exodus 19:13 we see God's intention that eventually the people come up the mountain. The mountain is never meant to be just a place for Moses and Joshua. In Exodus 24 we see the elders going up the mountain, but the people are not allowed to come. I wonder why this is? I suspect that God knew they weren't ready; God knew that they hadn't really engaged with the process of consecration. God is a holy God, a God not fooled or hoodwinked. The Israelites were not ready for an encounter with the Most Holy God because they were not prepared.

God's heart is not for one or two select people to ascend the mountain; God's heart is for the multitudes to climb the mountain. It is our choice, not God's plan that causes us to climb the mountain or stay at the base. Joshua was ready to hear the ram's horn—his ears strained, his heart excited. When Moses said, '*Come*,' he was there, he was ready, he didn't even need the horn. Are we straining to hear the ram's horn, the call of *time* on the plans and purposes God has ordained for us.

5.   *The place of revelation*

In Exodus 20–23 Moses receives revelation on the law, the people, and the future promise. He is then sent to collect Aaron, Nadab, and the seventy elders. I wonder what Joshua was doing when Moses was receiving revelation? I suspect he was seeking God for revelation as well. Sometimes in life we go though seasons of things being hectic and we live in the day to day of what God is doing. Sometimes we go through quieter times, times of less pressure. These are times to seek the Lord. How do we use the quieter seasons of our lives? The things that we sow into our lives in the quiet times come back in the noise and the more stressful times to encourage us and minister to us, if we sow nothing in we can expect to have a small reservoir to draw on. Proverbs 19: 8 states that "*He who gets wisdom loves his own soul; he who cherishes understanding prospers.*" If you cherish something you treasure it, you value it, and you attach great importance to it. To cherish the understanding of God is to value and deepen that understanding so that when we look for our treasure, our jewels in the darkness, we find a beautiful hoard, a deep reservoir.

6.   *The position of isolation*

In Exodus 24 the elders go up the mountain with Moses, they sacrifice, read the book of the Covenant, see a vision of God, and feast. They share an intimate meal with God. The elders are instructed to wait (Verse 14) until Moses and Joshua return as they are going on further. Moses and Joshua are together for seven days before God calls Moses into a cloud; Moses is then in the cloud for forty days and forty nights. Joshua is on his own.

The first thing to note is the disobedience of the elders; they didn't stay where they were. It's almost like they feasted until the food ran out, waited for a while, and then panicked. In their panic they dismissed the instruction of the man of God and cultivated their own solution. Moses had said he would be back, but his length of departure didn't meet with their expectation. In their stress they missed the plan of God and as a result, more than three thousand people died. If only they had stayed on the mountain.

Mountain top experiences are for a season—only it is God who determines the season, not our agenda. For the elders the mountain top experience became a place of death and disappointment, that was never its intention. The intention was an appointment with God, feasting with the creator.

For Joshua the mountain top experience was a life-changing moment. He was totally isolated. Because of his total isolation, I believe he came to know God as his provider, the one who fed him; as his company, the one who talked to him; as his comfort, the one who cared for him; as his security, the one who kept him. I wonder how Joshua felt when he saw or heard the elders jump ship back to base. Other people's disobedience did not make him question his appointment, he stayed where he was and didn't try to chase them back down the mountain. The elders presumed Joshua dead. It was the opposite, he had gone higher than they had.

The only way to stay in the place of appointment is to be in the place of revelation. I believe Joshua kept saying to God, 'Show me, show me'—that was the only thing that could have kept him in the right place. God is the one who takes us up the mountain and God is the one who brings us back down. Why did the elders come back down? Had they finished the feast? They missed the bigger feast! Joshua could have despised the place of isolation. He could have said to himself, '*I'll go and find the elders, check on the people.*' He would have missed out if he had.

Sometimes we need to be in the place where it is just God and us. When God calls us to a place of isolation, we need not despise his season. A place of isolation is a place where we learn to hear God in new ways and lean into him. No other person should take the place of God in our lives, he is our source. We live safe in the knowledge that God does not leave us in a place of isolation but he draws us to the next season of our lives. The reality is that we are never isolated because God is always there. Psalm 139 talks about the depths of God's love and how we can't escape it. Jesus experienced total isolation so that we would never need to.

Sometimes there are seasons of our lives in which we stand alone on the mountain, we need to learn to stay and be still in a place of mountaintop revelation, to pray with the psalmist, *"My heart says of you 'seek his face,' your face, Lord, I will seek"* (Psalm 27: 8).

Joshua was a man who stood on that mountain, and I have a feeling that on the mountain top he saw the land that God would give his people, he saw new things in the plans and purposes of God, and he saw himself in a new way. It is interesting that we are not told what Joshua saw—that was something he held in his heart. What are we looking for when we stand on the mountaintop with God? If we are looking for answers to our agendas, we will end up climbing back down—you don't find those on the mountain!

It is time to take in the mountain view, appreciate the heights, herald the revelation, and see the view!

CHAPTER 5

The Heart of a Worshipper

"Then the Lord would speak to Moses face to face as a man speaks with his friend. Then Moses would return to the camp, but his young assistant Joshua son of Nun did not leave the tent." Exodus 33: 11

Joshua was a man who looked to be in the right position—he was looking to be found in the right place. The scripture is given just after the incidence of the golden calf, and a plague has struck the people. God has told his people to move on but said that He isn't going with them. The atmosphere in the camp is heavy with uncertainty and guilt as Moses goes into the tent of meeting to seek the Lord for them.

"Now Moses used to take a tent and pitch it outside the camp, some distance away, calling it the 'tent of meeting,' anyone enquiring of the Lord would go to the tent of meeting outside the camp. And whenever Moses went into the tent, all the people rose and stood at the entrances to their tents, watching Moses until he entered the tent. As Moses went into the tent, the pillar of cloud would come down and stay at the entrance, while the Lord spoke with Moses. Whenever the people saw the pillar of cloud standing at the entrance to the tent, they all stood and worshipped, each at the entrance to his tent. The Lord would speak to Moses face to face, as a man speaks with a friend. Then Moses would return to the camp, but his young assistant Joshua son of Nun did not leave the tent." Exodus 33:11

The first thing that struck me about this scripture was the access into the tent of meeting. Notice the statement, 'anyone enquiring of the Lord.' There are no restrictions given; gender, age, race, etc, do not disqualify us from intimacy with God. Paul writes in Galatians 3: 28, *"There is neither Jew nor Greek, slave nor free, male nor female, for you are all one in Christ Jesus. If you belong to Christ, then you are Abraham's seed, and heirs according to the promise."* The promise of God extends over every individual who will receive his grace.

For me the *anyone* in this passage sparked the question, where was everyone else? Had they allowed the enormity of what had just happened to prevent them from dwelling in the presence of God? When we allow guilt to separate us from the presence of God, we place ourselves in a position of condemnation and isolation. It is important to understand the difference between conviction and guilt. Conviction is a work of the Holy Spirit; it highlights areas in our lives that we need to change so that God can have his way. Conviction is for kingdom purpose. Guilt is the enemy reminding us of things God has forgiven, if we allow it, it will disable us from being effective in God's kingdom plan—exactly what the enemy had in mind! Conviction should lead us to repentance—a place inside God's purpose; guilt (if we choose to carry it) leads us to isolation—a place outside God's purpose.

I wonder how many of the Israelites looked on Moses and Joshua with longing in their hearts and thought 'I would love to be there, if only I could be in that place.' I wonder how many of them watched with a disappointment in their hearts crying inside, 'If only I hadn't got it so wrong, if only I'd listened and waited.' How often do we do the same thing? It is so easy to look at people we esteem and think, If only I could have an anointing like that. If only I could hear God like they do. Guess what? You can. God does not have favourites—we are all his favourites. When we are looking at other people in awe of what they have in God, we should know that the same is there for us. If you want to hear God more clearly then you have to spend more time with him; if you want God to do miracles then you have to be in situations that need miracles.

Nothing in our past can prevent God using us, unless we allow it to. Look at Paul, a man with a very dodgy past. He was responsible for genocide against the Christian church—a religious extremist who thought his actions were the will of God. Paul stood by at the stoning of Stephen, giving his approval.[11] Yet Paul was totally transformed when he met Jesus on the road to Damascus, he went on to preach the gospel with authority, to see people healed, raised from the dead, released in the spirit, he became an apostle to the churches—he became their spiritual father. Paul knew the cost, because the original disciples first rejected him because of his previous reputation,[12] and then he suffered prison and torture. He wrote to the church in Corinth of his suffering, stating, "*I have worked much harder, been in prison more frequently, been flogged more severely, and been exposed to death again and again. Five times I received from the Jews the forty lashes minus one. Three times I was beaten with rods, once I was stoned, three times I was shipwrecked, I spent a night and day in the open sea, I have been constantly on the move. I have been in danger from rivers, in danger from bandits, in danger from my own countrymen, in danger from the Gentiles; in danger from the city, in danger from the country, in danger at sea; and in danger from false brothers. I have laboured and toiled and have often gone without sleep; I have known hunger and thirst and have often gone without food; I have been cold and naked. Besides everything else, I face daily the pressure of my concern for all the churches.*" (2 Corinthians 11: 23b–28)

Paul didn't allow his preconversion life to disqualify him from the ministry God had appointed for him. Our past will only disqualify us if we allow it. Next time we look at someone and hunger for what they have in God, we need to turn our hearts, our eyes towards God, we need to ask him for his abundance for our lives and be prepared to hear the answer. Expect to be stretched! If you pray for more faith, God will put you in situations where you need faith. If you pray for

---

[11]See Acts 8: 1–3
[12]Acts 9: 26–28

salvation, God will put you in situations where you need to share your testimony.

When we disqualify ourselves, we place our pride over God's purpose. When the Israelites stood and watched other people access God's presence, they were effectively telling God, 'This isn't for me, this isn't where I want to be, and I can't go there'—that confession eventually became their life. They didn't access the Promised Land because they had never learned to be secure in the presence of God; they had never learned to trust him or to really believe in his promises. The barrier of disqualification became an obstacle so big that it prevented them living in their inheritance. God does not call us to a half-life, he lays out our inheritance as a promise before us—we erect our own barriers or we take them down.

For me the difference between Joshua, Moses, and the rest of the Israelites was a difference of recognition and relationship. The Israelites operated in a place of recognition, they realised something was going on. They saw the pillar of cloud, they even worshipped outside their tents, and they had an understanding that awesome things were happening. They had grasped something of the holiness of the presence of God. I believe that the air was so tangible with God's glory that they didn't dare do anything but worship! But it stopped there; they never understood that God wanted a relationship. I look at Joshua and I imagine him in the tent of the meeting, crying out to God, *'God what do you have for me? What do you want to say to me?'* Even when Moses left the tent Joshua stayed where he was because he enjoyed being in God's presence.

We can recognise God, we can worship God, and we can know and understand things about him without being in a relationship with him. If I was to visit Buckingham Palace I would recognise the Queen straight away. I even know a few things about her—enough to expound a bit if there are any tourists around! I can curtsey and show her the respect her position affords but I don't have a relationship to her, I just know who she is from the things I have gleaned. We can be the same with God – we can recognise him, talk about him, be there in worship, but not have a relationship with him. Jesus didn't die on the cross simply so I could acknowledge Him, he died on the cross so that I could have a relationship with Him. Isaiah 53 states *"Come, all you who are thirsty, come to the waters; and you who have no money, come, buy and eat! Come, buy wine and milk without money and without cost. Why spend money on what is not bread, and your labour on what does not satisfy? Listen, listen to me, and eat what is good, and your soul will delight in the richest of fare. Give ear and come to me; hear me that your soul may live. I will make an everlasting covenant with you."* (Isaiah 55: 1–3)

Can you hear the heart of God? It is time to stop standing in a place of disqualification and to stand next to the king.

Joshua was a man who craved a deeper relationship with God. Joshua stood side by side with Moses and saw the anointing that Moses had and the authority that Moses carried, and he wanted the things he saw. Moses life was marked by encounters with the holiness of God, for example—the burning bush (Exodus 3), The Passover (Exodus 12), and Mt Sinai (Exodus 19–31). Moses was a man who saw God clearly, who came down the mountain with such a radiant face that the people couldn't look at him (Exodus 34: 29–35), yet Moses was also a man who knew a deep intimacy with God. Deuteronomy 34: 10 states that *"... no prophet has risen in Israel like Moses, whom the Lord knew face to face."* Moses walked with God closely, he knew the awe, and he knew the intimacy, and the two were a powerful combination. For Moses his burning bush experience marked a turning point, confronted with the holiness of God and the instruction to return and face his past, for the sake of his and his people's future, he tried to argue with God but then realised that he needed to obey. I believe if Moses had walked away from the burning bush then every bush he came across would have been burning until he responded. God is looking for encounters with his people, not distant encounters, but intimate encounters.

In Isaiah 6: 1–8 we see Isaiah encountering the holiness of God; his initial response is a cry of *'I am ruined, for I am a man of unclean lips!'* (Isaiah 6: 1–8). This changes to *'Here I am, send me'* (Isaiah 6: 8b). Here was a man who stood in the holiness of God, realised who he was—stripped of himself he saw the grace of God, and I believe it changed the rest of his life and his ministry. I imagine a paraphrase of Verse 8 that says *'Nothing in me wants to go, but I am so aware of who you are, so in awe of what you've done that I can't just simply stand here anymore, choose me, send me, and I will do what you will because I have seen who you are.'*

When we experience the holiness of God, our agendas become as dust. I don't believe Joshua ever said to God, 'I'd like to lead this people!' I believe as he worshipped in that tent, God so moved his heart that he was prepared to do whatever God wanted. Joshua was never going to be another Moses; Deuteronomy 34: 10 tells us that there was never anyone like him again. Joshua's anointing was different; primarily Joshua was a man of worship, a man who spent time seeking and searching the will of God. I find it really interesting that the battle tactic for Jericho was to walk around the city and then shout and blow trumpets 'at the sound of the trumpet there was a shout, and at the shout the walls gave' (Joshua 6: 20). Joshua's worship was an anointing that pierced the very core of those wall's foundations, which brought an entire city to rubble. In the face of such anointed worship, those stones never had a hope of standing, of holding up that city!

We need to cultivate an attitude of worship in our hearts, worship that defies circumstance and situation. No one made Joshua stay in the tent after Moses had left, he didn't have a time sheet on which he ticked off the amount of hours he had spent inside! God is looking for worshippers who simply delight to be in his presence and who long just to spend time with him.

When we worship God our lives line up with a position of worship, our problems line up with God's perspective. I have found one of the best places to worship God is in my car. On more than one occasion I have gotten into my car in tears as I have left people who I love, or during difficult situations, and I have sung through my tears down the motorway. I have always found that as I lift my eyes to focus on God I begin to see Him at work in the situations I have left, I find I know how to pray, that God gives me insight, and that my heart comes back to a place of peace. How awesome that something that starts off as a gift to God becomes something that comes back as a blessing to us.

Sometimes our worship is a sacrifice of praise. I wonder what motivated Joshua to be in the tent? Remember the situation he had just faced, the coming down the mountain to chaos. It would have been very tempting to have gone and hidden in his tent and prayed for the wrath of God to smite them! Instead he chose to place himself in the tent and worship. We can always worship God for who he is, we can remind our hearts of our salvation; of the things he has done for us. When we choose to place ourselves in the position of worship, we are placing God's agenda over our plan, heaven over earth, supernatural over natural—it is an invitation to heaven to move.

When I was off work with depression, I attended church on a Sunday. My life felt like I was a disaster, and I didn't really want to be alive. I remember standing in church, singing the songs, not feeling a thing, but knowing there was power in the words I was declaring. A couple of months later God healed me and I was back at work. Worship is a powerful place.

Psalm 84 talks about the beauty of being in God's house and the psalmist writes, *"Better is one day in your courts than a thousand elsewhere; I would rather be a doorkeeper in the house of my God than dwell in the tents of the wicked."* (Psalm 84: 10).

It is time to inhabit the place of praise again, to learn what it means to dwell in the courts of the Lord, to be found in the tent worshipping when everyone else has gone. It is a beautiful thing to linger in the presence of God. The psalmist talks about being hidden under the shelter of God's wings.[1313] Under the shelter of God's wings is an intimate place, not a corporate place. Our worship with God comes from our intimate times with him, our times alone where we simply adore the king. I remember at university being so frustrated that every time I set out to have some time with God, the phone would ring, eventually I unplugged the phone! It takes determination to find time with God; people invade, life invades, circumstances invade, but the invitation of heaven is always there.

I also believe that Joshua was a man who understood the future. He knew that one day he would have to lead these people. He wouldn't always stay in the role of the assistant. Joshua recognised that the things we sow into our lives are the things we draw on when the going gets difficult. Some of the key scriptures I remember are scriptures I learned as a child in summer camps. We called them memory verses and we used to say them every morning and evening meeting and to our tent leaders. As I became older, I was a tent leader myself and devised actions as a way of ensuring that I would remember the verses as well! I didn't realise it at the time, but these scriptures became key verses in my life. Every year John 3: 16 would come back again and again—what a fantastic base-line to have in your life![14]

Joshua was a man who understood the importance of sowing good things into his life; his worship was a lifestyle choice. What is our lifestyle choice? Are we choosing a lifestyle of worship? Do our lives reflect an adoration of the king? The Westminster Catechism says: *"The chief end of man is to glorify God and enjoy him forever."* We worship God first; we make it our mission to lift him as high as possible. When Jesus rode into Jerusalem, the Pharisees commanded him to quieten the crowd. I imagine Jesus almost laughing as he

---

[13]Psalm 36:7

[14]"For God so loved the world that he gave his one and only Son, that whoever believes in him shall not perish but have eternal life." John 3: 16

responds: *"I tell you, if they keep quiet, the stones will cry out."* (Luke 19:40). The book of Psalms states: *"The heavens declare the glory of God."*[15] I don't want a stone to cry out in my place, a star to speak of God's glory instead of me. I want to be found as a worshipper.

---

[15]Psalm 19:1

Heart

What does it say?
If a stone cries out in my place,
What does that declare?
Of the beauty of your grace,

If I don't sing
Will a star sing out my song?
Will it bring a melody of majesty?
With some notes right and others wrong,

Could it be?
That if I refuse, if I steal away
The rocks on the road
Will dance in praise,

How can I be?
A silent voice,
A withheld tune,
A muted noise,

My heart explodes,
A sacrifice of praise,
A pouring out of gratitude,
My Saviour, all my days.

CHAPTER 6

A Man of Adventure

"Then Caleb silenced the people before Moses and said, 'We should go up and take possession of the land, for we can certainly do it.'"

In Numbers 13 we read about the adventures of Joshua and Caleb as they go to explore Canaan, the Promised Land. Out of twelve spies who are sent, Joshua and Caleb are the only ones to bring back a positive report; they are convinced God will give them the land. They are overridden by the other spies who scare the people with talk of all the problems that face them, comments like *'the land we explored devours those living in it.'* (Numbers 13: 32b). As a result Numbers 14 sees Joshua and Caleb overruled and God's judgement pronounced. Joshua and Caleb alone will see the Promised Land and everybody else over the age of 20 will perish in the desert.

Joshua was a man who put his life on the line more than once. As a spy in enemy territory, it is likely that if he had been caught he would certainly have been captured and probably tortured and killed. The spies were chosen because they were leaders in their tribes; I wonder what their response was to being chosen? I can see some of them being proud and determined, others fearful and not pleased, and others full of the best way to explore the land. I wonder how many of them really prepared themselves for the task that was ahead. Looking at Joshua and Caleb we see their steadiness, but their living on the edge separated them from their compatriots. Let's look at things that set Joshua and Caleb apart.

1.   *They were already leaders.*

When Moses came to choose twelve leaders, I imagine the names of Joshua and Caleb came quite naturally to him. Who better to explore the land that his young assistant and his friend who he spent so much time with? These men were natural choices because they had cultivated lifestyles and attitudes that simply declared, 'God first.' Paul writes about those who are overseers in God's work stating that *"Since an overseer is entrusted with God's work, he must be blameless—not overbearing, not quick-tempered, not given to drunkenness, not violent, not pursuing dishonest gain. Rather he must be hospitable, one who loves what is good, who is self-controlled, upright, holy, and disciplined. He must hold firmly to the trustworthy message as it has been taught, so he can encourage others by sound doctrine and refute those who oppose it.'*[16] It is almost like these verses were written to describe these two men! If we aspire to lead other people, we must live a life that is worthy of an overseer. Does that mean we don't make mistakes? No, we are human and it is inevitable that we will, but it means we keep our eyes on God, His way and His rule. One of the best things we can do in life is to hold firmly on to the things that God has told us, this then acts as a benchmark for us, a benchmark of God's truth that accepts all that is good, receives and gives encouragement but throws out anything that is contrary to God's word.

If Joshua and Caleb hadn't gone as spies, chances are that they would have perished with the rest of the over twenties in the desert. They could have 'let someone else go,' or 'given someone else a chance.' Joshua and Caleb have such an understanding of God's heart that I believe they probably knew their names were going to be called before they were. How do we respond when God calls our name? Are we like Joshua and Caleb—are we ready to go?

---

[16]Titus 1: 7–9

2.   *They went to fulfill a clear commission; they went to find out the answer to important questions.*

When I first read this passage I had an image of Caleb as a kind of gung-ho soldier, wielding his sword around shouting, 'Let me at them, I'll show them a thing or two.' I imagined him charging off into Canaan without a look behind him, leaving Joshua to catch him up. When I read the passage more clearly I saw differently. This was a detailed commission; they were dispatched with a series of questions that needed answering: Good or bad land? Strong or weak people, fortified or unwalled towns, fertile or poor soil, trees and fruit? (Numbers 13: 19–20). This was no time to go charging into situation and cause chaos, they needed to run with the strategy of heaven.

Sometimes we receive a commission from God and charge in straight away without a thought for the outworking. If Joshua and Caleb had done this, the consequences could have been catastrophic. When God tasks us with something, he has a way of achieving that task. God's heart is to be intimate with us, to have conversation with us; he wants to give us strategy. Sometimes we need to go back to God with the commission he has tasked us with and ask the right questions.

3.   *They went to bring something back.*

Joshua and Caleb had no expectation of returning empty-handed, not content with just bringing back some grapes; they also managed pomegranates and figs! (Numbers 13: 23). Joshua and Caleb wanted to come back with the best of the fruit; it must have taken quite some effort to carry a pole with fruit hung on across the border! I don't believe that it would have occurred to Joshua or Caleb to return empty-handed. I imagine them looking for the best pieces of fruit, things they could take back to the people as proof of how good this land was.

There is a wonderful praise song that states 'I went to the enemy camp and, took back what he stole from me.'[17] Sometimes part of our commission is to reclaim things that were ours. The gospel of John talks about the enemy as a thief and a robber. John 10:10 says, *"The thief comes only to steal and destroy; I have come that they may have life, and have it to the full."* The good news is that through Jesus we have the key to everything the thief has stolen, he has no power to keep anything from our grasp.

When Caleb and Joshua plucked the fruit from the trees, it was also a prophetic declaration, 'we are coming back, and this will be our land.' When we understand the strategy of God, we can do the same things in our lives. *'I'm taking this because I know that God has this for me.'* John Chapter 10 talks about the shepherd and the thief. We can make the mistake sometimes of according the shepherd and the thief the same status, and they are not equal. The shepherd is the gate, the key holder, and the one ahead and behind, the security, the sacrifice, and the authority. The thief can only get in by climbing over a wall somewhere; he has no keys, only the power of persuasion. The thief has no comeback when God's people move in his strategy, purpose and plans.

4.   They went to explore, they were looking for the victory.

I imagine Joshua and Caleb spying out the land and I imagine them looking for ways in, asking the questions, which walls are guarded? What is the best way of overcoming their army? Which way in will give us the most surprise? I believe that when Joshua and Caleb were exploring they were looking for the victory. I imagine them hatching battle plans late into the night. Their mindset was a mindset of victory; their question was, how do we do this? There is a fantastic chorus

---

[17]'I went to the enemy's camp song' Words and Music by Richard Black 1991 (CCLI Song ID #467628).

we sing at church that declares: "All Things are Possible."[18] As we sing these words, you can almost feel faith rise around the building. Declarations like this remind us of who God is, of the miracles he has done. Caleb and Joshua had watched the Egyptian Army drown, they knew what God was capable of. If God could do that, he was more than able to deal with a few Nephilim (Numbers 13: 33).

The other spies I imagine running from tree to tree in a cold sweat cursing Moses. I imagine them asking each other doubtfully, *'can we do this?'* Can we? is a question that can destroy our hope because, more often than not, we can't, we aren't supposed to. The ability to perform the miracle is with God; the privilege of standing in the miracle is ours.

A miracle is not something we can work out and then produce ourselves; a miracle is a sovereign act of God that overrules the natural circumstance. Joshua and Caleb recognised the miracle provision they lived in, and looked for that same miracle provision, as they explored they wondered about strategy—how would God do? They allowed themselves to become excited by the impossible.

We need to be a people who look for the victory, who recognise and look for the miracle provision of God. We need to be a people looking both for the miracle and the strategy.

5.   They said yes in the face of other people's no's.

There is something awesome in the confidence that these two men display as they stand before the whole Israelite assembly and try to persuade them that the land is theirs.

"Joshua, son of Nun, and Caleb son of Jephunneh, who were among those who had explored the land, tore their clothes and said to the entire Israelite as-

---

[18]Almighty God, My Redeemer, Darlene Zschech, Hillsongs Church, Australia. 1996

sembly, 'the land we passed through and explored is exceedingly good. If the Lord is pleased with us he will lead us into that land, a land flowing with milk and honey, and will give it to us. Only do not rebel against the Lord. And do not be afraid of the people of the land, because we will swallow them up. Their protection is gone, but the Lord is with us. Do not be afraid of them.' But the whole assembly talked about stoning them."

Numbers 14: 6–10.

You can almost hear the questions that are not voiced, *"Do you know what you are doing?" "Don't you realize? This is our time!"* The people saw only the obstacles, but they saw probable war and death. Caleb and Joshua saw the promise—deliverance and life. The circumstance was the same. In every circumstance there is the grace of God to see victory and deliverance.

God's glory always follows his yes—in Numbers 14: 10b–35, the glory of God appears at the Tent of Meeting and God talks with Moses. In this conversation, there is judgement for the people (forty more years of wandering) and a promise for Caleb and Joshua that they alone, of the over twenties, would see the Promised Land. The yes of God is a serious thing; if Joshua and Caleb had given in they would not have received the inheritance that was there for them. I believe Joshua and Caleb had also caught something of the holiness and awe of God, they knew that God, in all his righteousness, would not be pleased at the way the Israelites were rubbishing his promise. In doubting the promises over them, in hoping to go back to Egypt, they were making a liar out of God. When Joshua and Caleb tore their clothes it was like an unspoken declaration—*'we want none of this.'* God saw the heart of Joshua and Caleb, a heart that believed and stood on the promise, a yes heart. God is looking for people with a *'yes'* heart, people who will stand on his word and look for the miracle answer.

6.   *They understood the power and the promise of God.*

Joshua and Caleb understood the power of God more than the rest of the spies. For Joshua and Caleb, that understanding of the power of God drew them into an intimacy with God. They understood that a God who demonstrated such mighty power on their behalf had a plan and a purpose for them; they longed to be closer to the One who would do such things for them. I believe for the rest of the spies the power of God frightened them; they saw what God could do and didn't want to get too close! The trouble is when we stand at a distance from God, other people have much more power to influence our decision making than God does, and when this happens our decisions don't tend to be that great.

The power of God should inspire both awe and intimacy. There is a holy fear in which we stand before God, but that holy fear should lead us to a place of intimacy. In Isaiah Chapter 6, Isaiah sees God. His initial response is the place of awe; a right fear of God. Out of that place God draws Isaiah to a place of intimacy where conversation takes place. God desires to have conversation with his people. If we want to understand the power of God we first need to understand the fear of God. The spies had a very real fear of the opposing army/city but not of God, a fear of God enables us to see God as bigger than our situations, it gives us a perspective that we otherwise can't find.

The power of God is our empowerer—the power of God is what enables us to fulfill the plan of God in our everyday lives. When we live in the power of God we begin to understand more of the promises of God. Walking in the power of God means we are more dependent on the promises of God because we are relying on the answer of God. When Joshua and Caleb looked at the land they were confident that God would give it to them so they were looking for heavens answer—they were already searching for the how. The rest of the spies were looking for some kind of confirmation—they didn't understand that the confirmation came from knowing who God was and what He had already said that they had already missed the confirmation and as a result saw nothing but difficulties that resulted in fear.

When we live in a right fear of God, we begin to understand the power of God. As we enable the power of God to empower us, we begin to realise more of the promise of God. Psalm 91 talks about inhabiting the place of power and we see in this psalm how in that place we see promises answered, *"If you make the Most High your dwelling – even the Lord, who is my refuge– then no harm will befall you, no disaster will come near your tent. For he will command his angels concerning you to guard you in all your ways."* (Psalm 91: 9–11)

God is longing for a people who run after his empowering, who live in his promises, who operate out of a right fear of God.

7.   They understood the timing of God.

In Numbers 14 we see a plague strike the other ten spies and they die. After this, the people are convicted and some decide to go and take the land after all, even when Moses tells them it is a bad idea. The result (fairly predictably!) is that they lose. I wonder how Joshua and Caleb felt? To explore the land and receive the yes from God, to see the people dismiss it, the judgement of the Lord fall and the instruction to keep wandering, and then for some people to rise up and try and take the Land after all. It must have been confusing. In Joshua and Caleb I see a confidence that recognises the voice of God. It would have been very easy to have their heads turned and think 'This is it!' and run with the others to fight the battle. The fact is Joshua and Caleb both received their promise (Numbers 14:24, 30) and they knew that they would see the Promised Land, just not now; they would have a forty-year wait.

It must have been a very hard thing to stand and watch those people run to fight a doomed battle. The people missed the heart of God; they went for the obedience without grasping that repentance was needed first. I wonder if they thought God would see their obedience and change his mind? God cannot be manipulated.

One of the things that amazes me about Caleb is his readiness. It was not his fault he got landed with another forty-year meander; but he chose to live in that season, to make sure that when the next season came he was ready. By the time he entered the Promised Land, he was ready to inhabit the moment and with absolute certainty he says to Joshua:

> "I was forty years old when Moses the servant of the Lord sent me from Kadesh Barnea to explore the land. And I brought back a report according to my convictions, but my brothers who went with me made the hearts of the people sink. I, however, followed the Lord my God wholeheartedly. So on that day Moses swore to me, 'The land on which your feet have walked will be your inheritance and that of your children forever, because you have followed the Lord my God wholeheartedly.' Now then, just as the Lord promised, he has kept me alive for forty-five years since the time he said this to Moses, while Israel moved about in the desert. So here I am today, eighty-five years old! I am still as strong today as the day Moses sent me out' I'm just as vigorous to go out into battle now as I was then. Now give me the hill country that the Lord promised me that day. You yourself heard then that the Anakites were there and their cities were large and fortified, but, the Lord helping me, I will drive them out just as he said."[19]

Talk about keeping your spirit ready! It would be so easy to be resentful but instead, Caleb makes sure that he is in the right place with the right attitude. He wanted that land. How

---

[19]Joshua 14: 7–12

much do we want the promises that God has for us? How ready are we to go through the seasons he has for us?

8.   *They were the only ones to see the Promised Land.*

Of a generation of people only Joshua and Caleb walked into the promise that God had given. In Exodus 15, Moses and Miriam sung a prophetic song which promised that God would *'plant them in the mountain of his* [God's] *inheritance'* (Exodus 15: 17). This was a promise for every person who crossed the Red Sea, not just for Joshua and Caleb, but I wonder how many people actually owned that promise; I wonder how many people allowed themselves to be robbed of the promise along the way.

We need to be a people who live in the promises of God, who choose to believe, and who confess and cling to those promises.

I want to be someone who is found holding onto the promises of God, to declare as Caleb did, *'Give me my land and I will live in all God has for me.'*[20]

---

[20]My paraphrase, Joshua 14: 12

Psalm 126: Caleb's Song

When I saw the Promised Land again,
As my wandering feet touched the dust of the land once
   more,
I began to live my dream,
I threw back my head and laughed,
And called to my brothers,
"Dance with me, sing with me, for I am filled with joy,"

"Precious God, restore our fortunes,
Like streams flowing with speed and precision,
So might we be."

"I sowed my words with tears and sorrow,
But here I reap my inheritance with songs of joy,
For he who goes out weeping,
Carrying hopes, dreams, many seeds,
Returns with proclamations of victory,
With sheaves of blessing."

CHAPTER 7

A Man Who Took
up the Mantle

*"Moses my servant is dead. Now then, you and all
these people, get ready to cross the Jordan River into
the land I am about to give to them – to the Israelites.
I will give you every place where you set your foot, as
I promised Moses."*

Joshua 1: 2–3

In Deuteronomy 34 we read that Moses climbs Mount Nebo,
sees the Promised Land for himself and then dies. After this
God digs the grave so that Moses bones are never found. The
Israelites knew this was going to happen and so mourn for
Moses for thirty days before God moves them on. I wonder
how Joshua felt as he watched Moses walk away, walk to
his death. I visualise Moses going with a sense of excitement—his earthly journey was over, his heavenly journey
was just beginning, and he was about to be reunited with
Aaron, Miriam, and his parents. No more deserts, no more
manna—he was going to feast!

Joshua's perspective would have been a bit different I
think—after all, he was about to lose the security of being
the understudy. He was facing the Jordan River with no con-
ceivable means of getting across it. Apart from Caleb, everyone was at least twenty years younger than him and the
people he was leading were not renowned for obedience and
trust! This was it. Was he ready? Would he ever be ready?
His whole life had been headed for this point and now he
was finally here.

Praise God that he doesn't wait for us to be ready; he readies us in the waiting. I love the illustration of the eagle teaching her young to fly, she carries them under her wing, ready for the time that the current is just right and the little wings are ready and then she lets go, watching her little one free fall in fright and then instinctively flap its wings and find to its surprise and delight that it is flying, really flying for the first time.

I wonder what would happen if you risk assessed the eagle's teaching tactics? In England we have something called OFTED that every school has to go through. A team of inspectors come into your school to grade every aspect of teaching, management behaviour etc, I wonder what OFSTED grade the eagle would get for her flying lesson? I have a feeling she might be in special measures! (The worst grade). I wonder what Health and Safety would say? God doesn't do risk assessments—he doesn't need to. He doesn't do things our way. His plans are designed to catch the perfect current, the furthest wingspan. The eagle chooses her moment, she doesn't just dump her young, she watches and waits for the right day—God does the same.

I look at this story and it seems harsh to me. Surely Joshua deserves an arm around the shoulders, or maybe even a bit of time team leading? Couldn't Moses have crossed the Jordan with him first? Instead God calls to him, *'It's over, this is enough. Arise, this is your time.'* It is no coincidence that Moses and Joshua both faced rivers to cross at the start of their journeys, the crossing of the river sealed their leadership. When the Nile went back into place there was no going back to Egypt, and when the Jordan went back into place the desert experiences were over. After walking through a river on dry land, the mark of God's anointing was clearly upon them.

Sometimes the way out of the desert is quicker than we think. We can spend time and energy looking at strategies, trying to get there, and feeling immensely frustrated when nothing works—sometimes it is time to consider the Jordan.

The ways that we rule out can be God's highway of opportunity. It is a miracle that moves us out of the desert and into the appointed position. Sometimes God leads us to the Jordan and we turn back to the desert thinking that we have gotten it wrong or that God has changed the plan—this isn't the case, *'we're going over the Jordan!'*

When I read the stories of Joshua, I see a man who took up the mantle—a man who ran with the words he had received. What does it mean to run with the mantle that God has passed to us? How do we receive the things God has and run with them?

1.   We stand close to the person from whom we receive the mantle.

Think for a moment of a 100-metre relay team. They spend ages in training, practising, ensuring that their handovers are swift and smooth. If one person drops the baton, the team is disqualified. I remember watching a heat at the Olympics—the USA were hot favourites. They had four amazing sprinters and no other team could match the kind of quality they displayed. They were on track to break the world record ... only the baton never made it round. They had their fastest sprinter on the last leg but he never even got a look in. What point am I trying to make? You've got to know how to receive the mantle or you'll never run with it successfully. You can run as fast as you like but, without the baton, you don't register in the race.

Joshua received a mantle passed to him from Moses. He had stood with Moses for years and always known this day would happen. Joshua had stood with Moses at the cost of his family, at the cost of his friendships (Caleb excepted), at a cost of isolation, at a cost of being delegated things he didn't really want. Standing close to Moses wasn't the easiest place to stand, but it was the right place. Only by standing next to Moses would Joshua see the things he needed to see, hear the things he needed to hear. Numbers 27: 12–23 talks about the time that Joshua will succeed Moses, and Moses is commanded to commission Joshua, and in commissioning Joshua he will give Joshua some of his authority (Numbers 27: 20). Note that Joshua isn't having all of Moses authority, he is having some of what Moses had and the rest is God's portion for him. Joshua is going places Moses isn't allowed to go—he is going to see victory that Moses couldn't have. In standing close to Moses, Joshua has received wise counsel, prophetic words but now he is pressing deeper in. The understudy is never simply the understudy, he won't always be the understudy, and when he plays the lead, he brings a whole new interpretation to the role. In order to receive the things God has and run with them, we need to stand close to the right people, not simply to imitate them but to press in deeper to what God has for us.

2.   We receive our commission from the right person.

Joshua received his commission from Moses—the man of God. He knew that commission meant that he would eventually be the leader of the Israelites. Numbers 27: 18–23 talk about Joshua's commissioning—it is a powerful time.

   Who have we received our commission from? I have news for you—we don't need to wait for one! We have all received our commission from Jesus in Matthew 28: 19–20. Jesus said: *"Go and make disciples of all nations, baptising them in the name of the Father and of the Son and of the Holy Spirit, and teaching them to obey everything I have commanded you."* Sometimes we can be waiting for a commission that we have already received, to make a disciple we don't even need to go to a nation, we can start with the nation we live in. We can also be very good at looking at the first part of the verse and ignore the second part. God isn't about just *'bums on seats,'* but about people walking in true obedience—true commitment. Half a commission is half a blessing; we can do ourselves out of full blessing by going on half measures. Commission always comes from a place of covering—it is a *co*-mission. Commission comes from God through the authority of his church.

There is no co-mission in being a lone ranger. Our co-mission comes in two parts; we are partnered with God. He has the ideas and we carry them out (the other way round isn't successful!). The second part of the commission comes from our sending authority, our church, it comes with accountability. In Luke 10, Jesus sends out the seventy-two, two-by-two, with clear instructions, and then they return to him. We need to be aware of whom we stand with in our commission and who we are accountable to.

3.   We start our journey with a word over our heads.

The start of Joshua's journey as a leader was marked out by a word, *'Moses my servant is dead'* (Joshua 1: 2). In other words, *'It is over.'* We start that journey with the same word over our heads. Romans 8: 1–2 states: *"Therefore, there is now no condemnation for those who are in Christ Jesus because through Christ Jesus the law of the Spirit of life set me free from the law of sin and death."* We do not need to live in the desert of our past experiences, the slate is clean and we make a new start with God. For Joshua the word over his head was a leaving behind, for him the role of understudy stayed in the desert and, in walking over the Jordan, he was walking into a new chapter of his life. Sometimes, God's word over our heads is obscured by other words that are over our heads—from other times and other places. There is only room for one word over our heads and we need to make sure that it is God's word. God's heart for his people is that we understand the word over our heads—it is a word that brings us out of the desert.

4.   We start our journey with a prophetic word.

For Joshua the prophetic word over his life was that *"At his [Joshua's] command he and the entire assembly of Israelites will go out, and at his command they will come in."* This was a word that gave Joshua something that Moses had never really had. Moses had battled continuously against the people coming up with their own ideas, everything from going back to Egypt to stoning him. This word told Joshua that he would rule with a different authority than Moses, there would be a unity that hadn't been there in the desert.

What is the prophetic word over our lives, what does it tell us? God is a speaking God; he is looking to input into the lives of his people, sometimes we don't receive God's counsel because we are not asking for it. I remember getting so frustrated that I felt I wasn't hearing God's voice, that I eventually made some space and sat with my journal, determined that I would carve out some time and get a response. I remember my first question, *'Where are you?'* And the gentle whisper of God responding, *'Where I have always been, right next to you.'* I realised that God hadn't stopped speaking to me but I had simply stopped listening. God is the same God; the same God who appeared and spoke to Moses, who gave that word to Joshua; the same God wants to give us a word. It is time to be a people who look for the prophetic over our lives, not simply so it's there, but so we operate in the fullness of what that means. God's prophetic word is always given for a purpose, not just to be there. The word over Joshua's life meant that he could operate in an expectation that the Israelites would move with him; it was a word for purpose. What is the purpose for the prophetic words over our lives?

5.   We walk in 'who we are' not in 'who somebody else is.'

Joshua knew he would never be Moses and that was never his aim. Moses did things that Joshua wouldn't do because they weren't part of his anointing. Moses was a singer, and we see him sing prophetic songs in Exodus 15 and Deuteronomy 32. He sings songs of exhortation, of prophetic declaration and of encouragement. Joshua never aspired to be a singer, that wasn't his way of communicating to the people, it wasn't something God used, but God used Joshua in different ways. Joshua fought battles, distributed land, and helped the Israelites settle in the new land, his was a different anointing. In the Promised Land Joshua's anointing was what was needed; Moses' anointing was for the desert place. If Joshua had tried to replicate Moses anointing, the people would have had a harder time settling in the land. Was there anything wrong with Moses songs? No. I suspect he was a gifted singer! But they were for a different season. Sometimes in life we are privileged to walk through seasons with anointed men and women of God, we learn from them, glean from them, but we should never try to be just like them—we are looking to be like Jesus. Joshua was confident in the anointing that God had for him; he was looking to God for his portion. We need to be a people who look for our portion, who look to run our race. In athletics if you run outside your lane, you are disqualified because you are infringing somebody else's race. The blessing and revelation you can receive from God are limited when you are in someone else's lane because they are not for you—God has a lane marked out, a race to run, a portion and inheritance set aside.

6.   *We walk with the wisdom of heaven.*

In Deuteronomy 34: 9 we read that Joshua received some of the wisdom that Moses had. I imagine that as Moses laid hands on him and prayed, Joshua began asking God, *'God give me a portion of his wisdom, I know I'm gonna need it!'* Joshua was a man who recognised what he needed; he wasn't tempted to ask for something else. In our lives we need the wisdom of heaven; the wisdom of heaven gives us God's perspective, God's answers, and God's heart. Proverbs 4:5–9 says, *"Get wisdom, get understanding; do not forget my words or swerve from them. Do not forsake wisdom, and she will protect you; love her, and she will watch over you. Wisdom is supreme; therefore get wisdom. Though it cost you all you have, get understanding. Esteem her, and she will exalt you; embrace her, and she will honour you. She will set a garland of grace on your head and present you with a crown of splendour."* Joshua knew the importance of wisdom; he understood what it meant to run after it. We need to be a people who understand the importance of God's wisdom. God's heart for his people is that they are wise and fruitful, that they look for his perspective and his answer. We find his answer in his word and in his voice, how well do we know his word? How clearly do we hear his voice?

Joshua was a man took up the mantle, a man who stepped out of a sad and difficult situation into his appointed place, he could have said, 'I'm too old, too sad, too unsure, too unprepared' but he denied every excuse available to him and picked up the mantle that he always knew he would carry. The same call rests over every one of our lives, Jesus himself declared:

> *"If anyone would come after me, he must deny himself and take up his cross and follow me. For whoever wants to save his life will lose it, but whoever loses his life for me will find it."* Matthew 16: 24–25

CHAPTER 8

A Man Who Crossed
the Jordan

*"When you see the ark of the covenant of the Lord
your God, and the priests, who are Levites, carrying
it, you are to move out from your positions and follow it. Then you will know which way to go, since you
have never been this way before."*

Joshua 3: 3–4

I will never forget the first person I led to the Lord. I was
fifteen years old and on a street evangelism camp. I had seen
God move miraculously in my life earlier in the week and
been baptised in the spirit for the first time. The team was
a group of dynamic young people on fire for God, and I felt
like I was seeing something so much deeper in God than I
had seen before. The team was divided into two, the dance
team and the drama team, and I was on the dance team. We
had learned two dances and would perform them on the
street, alternating with the drama team who had learned
various skits. When we weren't performing, we were partnered with another person from our team, and we were instructed to walk around the crowd and talk to people—trying
to engage them in conversation. We all wore bright yellow
T-shirts (and I mean bright yellow!) and we were full of the
amazing things God had been doing that week. My partner
Hannah and I wandered round the crowd and saw a man on
his own—watching. We approached him and started talking.
Hannah shared her testimony, exactly the same conversation that she'd had as a practise run with an older member
of the team earlier on. The man listened and then decided to

commit his life. We were both thrilled but suddenly unsure of what to do! We instructed the man to wait and ran to get our leader who came and led him to the Lord.

Why have I shared that story here? Well, for me, looking at the experience now is like watching a video in my memory. I see Hannah and me just pouring out what God had done for us, totally convinced God was moving. When we stand in the perfect will of God, impossible situations become opportunities for God to show his glory. I think of Peter walking on the water in Matthew 14—striding over the waves was his right place. Peter gets a lot of stick for starting to sink and not enough credit for being the only one to walk across the waves. The perfect will of God is the most natural place for us to be—not necessarily the easiest place or the most comfortable place or even the happiest place, but a place of depth with God that is only found in that place of total obedience.

There was nothing in Hannah and me that day that was particularly proficient at explaining the gospel; there was no ability in Peter that enabled him to stand on top of those waves, but simply hearts that longed to be where God was. For the rest of my life I will remember that day, an experience that told me right at the start of my ministry that when we step out in obedience, with a heart that simply longs to follow God's plan, he will do amazing things through us. For the rest of his life Peter would remember that he walked on water. He learned from the experience—of course he did—but he would never forget that feeling of standing on top of the storm. That moment was (I believe) a life-changing one for Peter, in getting out of the boat again he was placing himself out of his comfort zone, outside of his experience, it was almost like a prophetic declaration of his life.

When Jesus first stepped into Peter's life he just wanted to be a fisherman—that was it. He wrested with God's calling on his life, he didn't understand the things Jesus asked of him, imagined if God had listened to the cries of his heart to just be a fisherman, a normal guy. I know that I am guilty of praying, "*God, choose somebody else, send somebody else, I've had enough.*" I have discovered that when I have nothing in me to give, that I can give of God's best. That when God leads me to the edge of the water, it isn't so that I can sink, but so that he can make a way.

CROSSING THE JORDAN

Joshua was a man who led his people into new territory, he was a man with a word over his life (Joshua 1) and a man commanded repeatedly to stand in the strength and courage of God (Joshua 1). He was a man who led a people of reputation (Joshua 2: 8–11). Yet he was faced with a river that was in flood and didn't lend itself to the entire Israelite company walking across. Joshua and Caleb had crossed the Red Sea with Moses but the rest of the company had been born in the desert, they had never seen anything like this before. At the very start of his leadership, Joshua is totally and utterly dependent on the sovereign hand of God; there is nothing in him that can make the waters of the Jordan pile up. In the natural, I believe Joshua was a gifted man, a strategist, and organiser. He was a man who walked in the prophetic revelation, but this wasn't about simply gifts, this was about miracles. Our gifts are not given to us to draw up contingency plans, to provide God with alternative means should he desire it! Our gifts are given to us to enable us to walk out the miraculous in God. Joshua's gifts enabled the Israelites to live in the Promised Land, but it didn't get them there, it started with a miracle. There is a lot of teaching around on '*practical Christianity*', '*how to hear God,*' '*effective prayer,*' *and* '*the best way to have a quiet time*'—and there is nothing wrong with that. These are things we need to help us, but what about the miracle power of God? I look at his word and I see every book peppered with instances of people healed, people delivered, and people asked to do things that seem crazy—building arks, tearing down altars. I see people struck with the holiness of God—miracle power. A nation cannot ignore a church that moves in miracle power. Our nations need churches that move in miracle power. It is time to be a people who walk in the miraculous, not for entertainment, not simply for show but in God's heart for his people and the nations.

1.   The crossing of the Jordan— a marking of the end

In Joshua Chapters 3 and 4 we see the crossing of the Jordan—the moving of an entire company of people into the promise that has been over their heads for a long time. It was the end of the desert experience. Joshua 3: 13 states, *"As soon as the priests who carry the ark of the Lord—the Lord of all the earth—set foot in the Jordan, its waters flowing downstream will be cut off and stand up in a heap."* There are important principles at work here; the first is that the ark goes first. The ark is symbolic of the presence of God. It is no good wandering haphazardly into situations and expecting God to honour our plans and strategies, the miracle power of God goes hand in hand with a walk of obedience. You cannot have one without the other. Joshua 1 talks about the prophetic words over the Israelites, Joshua 2 talks about the preparation required before the miracle, the things that needed to happen in the natural, and Joshua 3: 5 talks about a time of consecration. This was no foolhardy adventure. This was a never again experience. The word was given to Joshua in Chapter 1 *"Get ready to cross the Jordan River"* (Joshua 1:2). Then there is a time of preparation, Joshua doesn't simply declare *'I'm off!'* and troop his people across. Sometimes things go wrong and we assume that the word we received was wrong, maybe we didn't hear quite right, or we missed something somewhere? Sometimes it is simply that we moved too soon. Joshua probably could have crossed the Jordan then and there but the people wouldn't have coped, they needed to understand the significance of what they were doing. When they crossed the Jordan, that part of the journey, that part of their lives was over. The waters would go back, they could never return to the desert, never go back to Egypt. Their entire way of living was about to become so very different. They were going from nomads to settlers, from wanderers to workers, from imagining the promise to living in the promise. The fire and the cloud would disappear and they would learn to see God in new ways. I believe that if they had charged across the Jordan, they would have tried to charge back again before very long.

What has God said over your life? Are you seeking the understanding of how to live in it? Joshua understood that there was a right way to cross the Jordan. Look at the order in Joshua 3—the ark is first (with the priests) and then after a safe distance the people follow. There is conversation between God and Joshua, the priests stand in the middle of the Jordan with the ark until everyone is crossed, memorial stones are sorted and then the priests finish their crossing with the ark. Notice the order in the miracle—the order is born of a confidence that the miracle will happen and that the miracle is a safe place. This is no race across the Jordan in case the waters fall back again. This is a hurried procession yes, but also an ordered one. The miracles of God are a safe place to stand in—the safest place. I remember Keri Jones (the apostle to our group of churches) saying that if God has called you to go to Iraq, then that is the safest place in the world for you to be. If he hasn't, you gamble with God's grace—that's an arrogant place to stand in. The miracles of God are a safe place. I believe that as the Israelites crossed the Jordan they saw the waters, they felt the sandy soil beneath their feet and they grasped the magnitude of what God was doing. They saw the memorial stones collected and something stirred in their hearts—the desert was over. These were a generation of children who had grown up on their parent's dreams and disobedience; they were living in and seeing something awesome.

The first thing Joshua does when he comes across the Jordan is set up the memorial stones—it is a marker. This was the start, this was what God did! How do we remember? What is our last point of reference? I'm not suggesting you collect a load of stones and build a memorial in your garden! For me, I always come back to that camp when I was fifteen. For the first time that week my Bible really came alive to me and promises leapt off the page. I still have my bright yellow t-shirt, even though I'm not sure I could wear it now! Every time I move to a new house it comes with me, and I am reminded that God met me, that he kept me, that in spite of everything that's happened since then, we keep journeying. I can't wear that t-shirt now; it would look a bit odd! But I live in the fruit of the season. Memorials are a joy and not a snare, a release and not a curse. If I look back to that time as the best of my life, I am in the wrong place and quite possibly the wrong church. It was a blessed time, but God has blessed me in new ways since. You don't settle in the place where you place your memorial.

2.   The crossing of the Jordan—a new order for a new time.

This time when the Israelites crossed the sea, they were following the ark. In Exodus 14 Moses stretches out his staff and the Red Sea divides and they all cross. During their time in the desert they had grown closer to God, they had received the law, built the ark, fashioned the tent, and learned the hard way about the holiness of God. This time the ark goes first. Notice that the priests have to get their feet wet before the waters move. In the presence of God the waters take the proper place, our circumstances resume their right position. The ark going first was God's plan for how the Israelites should live. When we became Christians we made a choice—God's way. As we walk more with him the order of our lives change— God goes first. We live in the confidence that God wants the best for us, so that even when his plans seems mad to us, we know that ultimately it will work out for his glory and our benefit. I reckon that if any of the Israelites had tried to cross the Jordan before the ark, they would have drowned. God was making a statement to his people – a clear statement. Me first. I love watching the film Evian Almighty.[21] I think it is wonderfully made. There is a scene at the end where Evian is talking to God and he says something like, '*You knew all along, but I fought you every step of the way, but if I hadn't done it that would have been my family, all those people . . .*' he stops as the magnitude of what he says hits him. There was no way he could have foreseen what would happen, but in the end a plan became clear and actually his 'sacrifice' in obedience became the deliverance for a lot of people. This is just a film, but the same principle applies in our lives. At no point does God promise he will reveal his complete master plan to us, but, at every turn we are assured of his promise over our lives. Jeremiah 29: 11–13 says: "*For I know the plans I have for you," declares the Lord, "plans to prosper you and not to harm you, plans to give you a hope and a future. Then you will call upon me and come and pray to me, and I will listen to you. You will seek me and find me when you seek me with all of your heart.*" When we said yes to God, we opened our lives up to a whole new order. It is time to ask again—what does that yes mean in my life? How does the order of my life reflect God's glory?

3.   Crossing the Jordan—a stepping into a new way of life.

Joshua knew that when the Israelites crossed the Jordan, things would never be the same again. The 'never been this way before' didn't just refer to the geography of the trip, it had a much wider implication than that. This was a generation that had only ever known the desert place, they had only ever eaten manna—now they would have access to all the good things of the Promised Land, including the vineyards and the crops. Their shoes had never worn out before,

---

[21]Evian Almighty—2007. Written by Ste Oedekerk and directed by Tom Shadya

now they would have to make their own shoes. They had always had the fire and the cloud before, now they would have to learn how to seek the direction of God. They had never worked before, now they would be farmers, labourers, builders, etc,—it was a whole new ball game. When God calls us into a new season it comes with a new equipping. If in the height of summer—beach weather, 30 degrees C (I live in hope!)—I wandered round in my big winter coat with hat, gloves, etc, I would attract some very strange looks because my winter clothes are not suitable for the summer season. The same principle applies in God. God has new things for us, new equipping for each season, a better change of clothes! On some James Bond-type action play station games the player moves up different levels. As he moves up he can acquire different weapons etc. He adds each weapon to his arsenal and builds up a collection, that way he has a choice of what to use. He needs these different weapons, because the further he advances, the more difficult the challenges he faces. Collecting the weapons and using them are a necessary part of the journey. If he doesn't, he will never progress. It is the same in God; standing still is not an option. God wants a people who advance—a people who are not stagnant, who run after all He has.

Paul writes in Philippians 3: 10–14, *"I want to know Christ and the power of his resurrection and the fellowship of sharing in his sufferings, becoming like him in death, and so, somehow, to attain the resurrection of the dead. Not that I have already obtained all this, or have already been made perfect, but I press on to take hold of that for which Christ Jesus took hold of for me. Brothers, I do not consider myself yet to have taken hold of it. But one thing I do: Forgetting what is behind and straining towards what is ahead, I press on towards the goal to win the prize for which God has called me heavenwards in Christ Jesus."* Paul knows what he wants. He wants to be closer to God. He recognises the cost of that but he knows the future is so much better than the past. Paul knew where he was headed and his intention was to take as many people with him as possible. He had no illusions about who he was or what he had; he simply knew the source and ran his race. Do we understand what it means to chase after the things of God? Sometimes we make things far too complicated. It is time to know who we are, time to run the next season of the race.

4.   Crossing the Jordan— the wandering was over.

Joshua 24: 13 talks about the new life the Israelites would lead—*"I gave you a land on which you did not toil and cities you did not build; and you live in them and eat from vineyards and olive groves that you did not plant."*

Their time of wandering was over, and it was time to learn to live a different way. When God takes something away, he replaces it with something else, something better. I bet the Israelites enjoyed their first meal that wasn't manna and I'm also sure that they never tasted anything quite like that manna again. For the Israelites to survive in the Promised Land, they had to learn new skills and I'm sure they weren't perfect straight away. Maybe they didn't gather the first harvest at quite the right time? Maybe some of the first buildings they built weren't great? There were probably some interesting clothes when they first had to make their own. Did this mean they were getting it wrong? They were just learning, taking baby steps in a new life. Sometimes we are easily discouraged because we think we have failed before we have even really tried. We need to remember that baby steps are an important part of the journey.

Sometimes people say things that are unhelpful and we sideline the gifts God has given us. The first time I played my saxophone in church somebody told me it was too loud (it was and probably off key as well!). Were they right or wrong—doesn't matter. What matters is our response. I didn't play my saxophone again in church for a long time, but I practised, I took exams, I just loved playing the instrument and when (finally!) I played it again, it wasn't too loud, it wasn't off key and God anointed it. Now, whenever I get the chance, I love to play my saxophone in worship. What's my point? My point is that Christianity is no cruise—we work at the journey. If I had put my saxophone down and never played again I would have missed out on the blessing of playing such an awesome instrument, of seeing God move through my playing. Should that person have said what they did? Doesn't matter—they were right! All I knew is that I had this heart to praise God, and I wanted to use the instrument that I loved. Did God mind the noise—no, he saw my heart, but deafening other people probably isn't the greatest advertisement for heaven's worship. I learned from it—I grew through it; I became a better player because of it. Too often we allow other people to distract us, sometimes with the best will in the world, and we miss what God is doing. There are a lot of Christians who wander, they wander from church to church, from experience to experience—the place of maturity is the place of a worker, not a wanderer. What do I mean by a worker? Somebody who works with all his heart at what God has called him to do. Wanderers break God's heart because it's second best—why wander when you can settle and see God move in new ways?

What does it mean to live in that place where you hear God and move? We can want the awesome experiences and hunger after them without actually being prepared to go out on a limb. God has a limb for all of us—it is his heart to take us there. It is not to completely freak us out but to experience the best of all He has for us. 1 Peter 1: 3–4 says *"Praise be to the God and Father of our Lord Jesus Christ! In his great mercy he has given us new birth into a living hope through the resurrection of Jesus Christ from the dead, and into an inheritance that can never spoil or fade—kept in heaven for you, who through faith are shielded by God's power until the coming of the salvation that is ready to be revealed in the last time."*

I want to be someone who runs for that inheritance and who takes as many people with me as I can.

CHAPTER 9

A Man Who Feared the Lord

Joshua was a man who lived in an understanding of the fear of the Lord, he recognised that if he wanted to see the sovereign hand of God at work he needed to be ready, watching, looking to see where God was moving and what his part was. Look with me at Joshua 5. The Israelites have just crossed the Jordan and they are preparing to move in on Jericho. Joshua 6 deals with the walls of Jericho falling but Joshua 5 is all about the preparation for taking the land. This is no scrum into Jericho, this is an appointed march into the prepared place; those walls were never given a chance of standing upright! It is no good just looking for God to do and seeing our role as chief spectator, we need to ask God where we are meant to be, what we are meant to be doing, and where we are meant to be praying. Sometimes we can view the miracle power of God as a spectator sport. We ask and we wait for God to 'do his thing.' This is not a Biblical view. A miracle starts with a word of God, an instruction to Noah, for example, to build the ark[22] or to Barak to ride out against the opposing army.[23] After the instruction comes action. In order for Noah to survive the flood he had to build an ark and then God shut the door and kept him safe. He could live in that miracle place only if he built the ark. For Barak to win the battle he had to ride out, only then God would move.

To live in a place of miracles is to live in the fear of God. Living in the fear of God surpasses everything else that we are afraid of, and it enables the sovereignty of God in situations that we hold dear to our hearts. Look at the contrasting

---

[22]Genesis 6: 14
[23]Judges 4: 6–7

attitudes of Deborah and Barak in Judges 4. Deborah knew she had heard the voice of God and the instruction was clear; she caught the victory, she was living in the victory before it was a reality. Barak, on the other hand, was living in a mindset of defeat—he had no confidence in the word that Deborah brought, appealing to her, saying, *"If you go with me, I will go, but if you don't go with me, I won't go."* (Judges 4: 8). Deborah has no hesitation in agreeing to go with him; after all she knows the battle is already won. Our lives would be different if we grasped hold of the truth of the promises of God. I believe the reason that Deborah stood out as she did was because she lived in the revelation that God gave her. She didn't care what people would say when she rode out next to Barak, because she knew that God was about to move mightily. Deborah was no maverick; she was a woman who moved in the anointing God placed on her, she had grown in her anointing and knew the power of walking out that anointing with obedience. Because God took centre stage in her life, she saw amazing miracles. We cannot expect to live and move in the miracle power of God. If we push God to the periphery of our lives, we need to live in a place where we understand more of the fear of the Lord.

What does it mean to live in the fear of the Lord? In Joshua 5 we see Joshua living in that place. For me there are four key things in this passage; the place of covenant, the release of testimony, the spiritual battle, and the place of awe.

1.   We live in Covenant.

The first thing that happens in Joshua 5 is circumcision. God tells Joshua to circumcise all the men who haven't been circumcised—i.e., everyone who had been born in the desert. Circumcision was a Covenant that God had made with Abraham in Genesis 17; it was God's promise that Abraham would be fruitful and the father of many nations. It set apart Abraham and his family and became the mark of the Jewish nation. Before the Israelites advanced into their new land, they needed to remember who they were; they needed to come back to that place of Covenant with God. In being circumcised it was like they were saying to God again, '*we belong to you.*' Circumcision was a place of obedience and a place of reminding themselves that they were God's. As Christian's, we are called to circumcise our hearts (Romans 2: 29). In our hearts we carry the identity of Christ and we live in the Covenant of the cross.

To live in the fear of the Lord is to live in the Covenant of the cross. The cross becomes my point of reference. In my time as a youth worker I was privileged to lead some youth alpha courses. Part of alpha looks at the cross and gives a description of what Jesus had to endure. For me, every time I read it, it brought home to me exactly what Jesus had done. I remember being told on a youth worker training course that if I was ever feeling distant from God, to go and shut myself in a room and read one of the gospel accounts of the cross. It's good advice. When did we become so familiar with the cross that we stopped appreciating the sacrifice that it cost? There is a beautiful old chorus that says very simply,

> I am not my own
> I've been brought with a price,
> Precious blood of Christ
> I am not my own,
>
> How could I ever say?
> I would choose another way,
> Knowing the price that's paid,
> I am not my own.[24]

I remember watching 'The Passion' for the first time. I cried pretty much all the way through, I think! I watched it with some women from church, and I remember wondering

---

[24]I Am Not My Own,"This is a song I used to sing in the early 1980's in the Assemblies of God Church, I have tried to source the author without success.

what was going on when at the end one of the women was laughing. She explained to us that watching the resurrection reminded her how awesome God was, that his power overrode everything—she saw the victory. Something in that changed my perception. We shouldn't come to the cross in complacency, but we don't come in misery either; we come in awe, in gratitude, but also in expectancy.

Every time we take communion we are reminding ourselves of the covenant God made with us, his body broken so I could be whole, his blood shed so I could be free. What is our approach to communion? Have we lost something of the fear of God? When we receive the bread and wine, we are taking into our flesh the victory over every circumstance that stands in our lives against God. It is time to receive that not just as a physical meal, but also as a spiritual truth. It is time to circumcise our hearts again.

2. We live in testimony.

After the Israelites had been circumcised, they celebrated the Passover (Joshua 5: 10). Their circumcision had been a declaration—this is how they would live in the Promised Land. They were going to walk out the Covenant that God had given them. In celebrating the Passover they were remembering their testimony and, in remembering their testimony, they were stepping into something new. When they celebrated the Passover, they were using the produce of the land for the first time, in consequence the manna stopped the day after (Joshua 5: 12). Our testimony exists not only as a reminder of the faithfulness of God, but also as a provocation to press deeper into the things of God. When we remember the miracles God has done, it should raise our faith. I was talking to someone at our cell group yesterday about how God had provided me a place on a teacher-training course back in 2004. This course had been the provision of God and had started in 2004 and recently stopped again. He had run only for a season. It had provided not only for me but also for the successors of my two secondary teaching jobs! God blessed not only me but was also faithful in providing for the secondary schools I taught in. As I talked, my faith for my friend's job/training began to rise. I remembered what God had done for me and it caused my faith to grow because there was no reason why God can't do it again for him.

Living in our testimony does not mean living in the past. Living in our testimony causes our faith to rise, it creates more testimony! I imagine that as the Israelites shared the Passover they recounted stories they had heard about the plagues, maybe Joshua and Caleb told them what it was like. I imagine them remembering the things God had done in the desert, the miracles of provision and healing they had lived through. Their faith rose. They were ready then to march on Jericho, ready to see what God would do. The trepidation of what might happen had become excitement. It is time to discover a right way to live in our testimony. Our testimony can be the key that unlocks faith for other people and that unlocks situations. We need to live in the place where we feed our faith on testimony.

David was a man who used his own testimony to raise his faith. In Psalm 103 he writes *"Praise the Lord, O my soul, all my inmost being, praise his holy name. Praise the Lord, O my soul, and forget not all his benefits—who forgives all your sins and heals your diseases, who redeems your life from the pit and crowns you with love and compassion, who satisfies your desires with good things so that your youth is renewed like the eagle's"* (Psalm 103: 1–5) His testimony spoke to his spirit, and it lifted him to a better place; a place where he could see clearly and move in God's anointing. How do we use our testimony? It is time to speak truth to our spirit in order that we rise to a better view.

3.   *We live in a spiritual battle.*

After the time of circumcision and celebrating the Passover, Joshua is visited by the commander of the army of the Lord. (Joshua 5: 13–15). He had taken the Israelites back to a place of covenant (through circumcision), and he was leading an expectant people, (inspired by testimony). He had cultivated an atmosphere that released something in the supernatural. What atmosphere do we cultivate in our daily lives? Are we expectant that the things in the spirit will touch the things of earth? When we live in the fear of God and the confidence of his promises, everything on earth has to give up its position to heaven's order. In Acts 16: 16–40 Paul and Silas (having been severely flogged) are in prison. It is midnight and they are having their own version of songs of praise. Everyone is listening—they have never heard anything like this before. There is no way that jail was ever going to hold them. There is an earthquake and the prison doors fly open and every-body's chains come loose. People who weren't even asking for freedom had found it because earth had to give up its order to heaven's agenda. Imagine having to explain that one to the prison authorities! When we align ourselves with heaven's answer and we move in that place of obedience, the things on earth have to give up their position because it is not an equal battle. If you want the things on earth to give up their power, you have to align yourself with the solution of heaven. When you fight flesh battles with flesh solutions you get flesh answers, when you bring heaven's answers to earth's problems you get heaven's resolution.

Joshua checks his source (Joshua 5:13) and then receives his answer (Joshua 5:14). He is about to receive heaven's an-swer to win this battle—an answer that will not cost him any lives in fighting or any injuries; it is a perfect plan.

What does it mean to live in a place of receiving the spiri-tual answers to our problems? We can look sometimes for a magic wand and be frustrated when there appears to be no answer. It is time to come back again to that place of cov-enant and testimony. If you are looking for heaven's answer in your life, can I encourage you to sit again with the cross, feed your soul on the things God has done in your life, re-mind yourself of the testimony you own, and allow God to grow and raise your faith for heaven's answer? The answer is there because the place of Covenant and testimony prepare the way for the place of encounter.

4. *We live in awe.*

When Joshua hears who his supernatural messenger is, he falls with his face to the floor and he is then given his first instruction, *"Take off your sandals, for the place where you are standing is holy,"* (Joshua 5: 15). This experience is significant; it is reminiscent of Moses calling in Exodus 3 when he is confronted with the burning bush. Why take off your shoes? I have a feeling that that was a prophetic declaration of taking off the way things were before. For Moses, he took off his shoes as a shepherd and put them on again as a leader and a prophetic voice. For Joshua, he took off the shoes of the desert experience and put on the shoes of his inheritance. In all the time in the desert their clothes and shoes had never worn out. Now they would start to wear out because it was time to live a new way. There was nothing particularly different about the patch of ground where the bush burnt or the place where Joshua stood, but it was made holy because it was the appointed place of God for that time of encounter and revelation. In taking off his shoes Joshua took off his comfort, his protection, and his journey. When he put them back on, something inside had changed.

To live in a place of awe is to live in a place of encounter—a place of walking without shoes! What do I mean by that? I don't mean that we go around barefoot. I simply mean that we are vulnerable before God. The place of encounter is the place of interrupted journey, of interesting strategy, and of living in heaven's answer. You can't expect heaven's answer if you are not prepared to take off your shoes. It is a declaration—*'There is nothing between me and this holy ground, no barrier, no cushion, no strategy, no clever idea, no nonsense, this is me.'*

I believe that when Joshua realized who he was speaking to there was no option but to bow. He knew in his spirit this was it. The answer of heaven is conclusive and it is perfect, it brings both an end and a new beginning. Joshua received the answer of heaven straight away because he was looking for it; he was ready to move into the next part of what God has. Sometimes we are so busy trying to negotiate with God that we miss out. God doesn't want to negotiate with his people, he wants to lead his people and that starts with being bare-foot. God in his grace gives us back our shoes! It is time to stand in awe again.

I Stand in Awe
I stand in awe in that holy place,
I tremble, as I know his grace,
I lift my eyes, to see his face,
And I am in love; yes I am in love,

And a song of worship stirs within my soul,
And a song of love overflows from my heart,
A song of joy is heard upon my lips
As I adore my lord,

Washed clean I stand before his throne,
Called by name I am his own,
I give my praise to him alone,
And I am in love; yes I am in love,

And a song of worship stirs within my soul,
And a song of love overflows from my heart,
A song of joy is heard upon my lips,
As I adore my lord.[25]

---

[25]I Stand in Awe, song written by Rose Starkey/Martyn Starkey, Kings Community Church, Lancaster, England.

CHAPTER 10

A Man of Strategy

"God takes you to the very edge of your gifting, the very limit of your skills and as you begin to accomplish more than you ever thought possible then he steps in with the miracle and our skills and abilities sit in their proper place, under the anointing of heaven in miracle provision." Beckie Jo Snell

Any major army general will tell you that Joshua's strategy for battle isn't a winning plan; they may even describe it as suicidal. Heaven's strategy often kicks against the way that we would work out things on earth. Sometimes, we make the mistake of thinking that God needs our helping hand, that maybe he didn't quite mean for us to do it that way. God's hands are all encompassing and our (often well-meaning) meddling can have unwelcome consequences in the plans and purposes of heaven. We can sing all the songs about surrendering to God and genuinely mean them, but what about when God calls us to do things that seem so completely crazy or utterly unworkable, what then? We wonder sometimes why heaven's miracles and earth's plans don't seem to line up. We can't present God with our plans and then ask for miracles. We go to God for his plans and live in the expectancy that as we are obedient and serve in his purposes so he will move.

If you are looking for a comfortable walk, you have missed something along the way. God takes us to the uncomfortable places, the places where we feel stretched, where we know we don't have the resources to meet what is required, because there we see the miracle provision of God. In the uncomfortable places we find an abundance of grace and truth that sustain us, love that holds us, we tap into new depths of the kingdom of God. I wrote my first book (a commentary on the life of Esther) during my first years of teaching. I carved out time most Wednesday evenings to sit in the word and write out the things that God had birthed in my heart. I found teaching difficult and, after spending my days policing teenagers, there were times when I felt simply exhausted. But in those times of drawing close to God I discovered an abundance and richness in His word that birthed a new excitement and depth in my relationship and walk with him. If I had stayed in my comfortable place (zone out DVDs!), I would have missed the things God had for me within that book.

To stay in the comfortable place and look for the miracle can prove to be a very frustrated place to wait. If you want to see miracles, you need to be prepared to live in the uncomfortable place.

In Joshua 6 we see a man who is looking to live in the miracle, a man of strategy. This was a man who understood and held the prophetic word close to his heart; who knew how to claim his inheritance, who knew the importance of God going first, who understood both the noise and the silence of heaven, and who knew the importance of obedience. Looking at Joshua we see a man who understands how to operate in a place of Holy Spirit strategy.

1.   *Joshua took hold of the prophetic word.*

In Joshua 6: 2–5 we see conversation taking place between the Lord and Joshua. Notice, first of all, that this was no gust of wind or impression on his heart; this was the real thing! God wants to be a God who is on speaking terms with his people. He wants to reveal his plans and purposes. What does it mean to be in conversation with God? Sometimes we can treat God a bit like the genie in the story of Aladdin—rub the lamp and then he appears and we ask for what we want. God doesn't play games with his people, and we need to understand that it should be the other way round. We are God's hands and feet on this earth, we wait for a word or instruction and then we move, we lean in to him and as we do so, we discover heaven's miracle power changing earth's situations.

What strikes me most about the conversation at the beginning of Chapter 6 is the normalcy of it; it is a very matter of fact thing! Joshua receives his instructions and goes on to instruct his army in what they will do. Notice that he doesn't question what God says, there is no *'Are you sure God?'* or *'What about this way?'* Joshua simply receives the word. What words have been spoken over our lives and how have we received them? Sometimes we can do a Jonah and receive a word, decide that we don't like it, and deliberately go off in another direction. Learn from the story of Jonah that if you do that, you are asking for a whale to bring you back again! Sometimes we receive a word and we get frustrated and try to bring about God's promises ahead of time, just look at Abraham and Sarah. We need to learn sometimes how to wait in the difficult times, Joshua after all had already waited years in the desert. Can I encourage you that if you are waiting on God for a promise he will fulfill his word in his perfect time, even when it seems like the time must have passed. God is not restricted by our definition of time. Habakkuk 2: 1–3 states, *"Write the vision and make it plain on tablets, that he may run who reads it. For the vision is yet for an appointed time, but at the end it will speak, and it will not lie. Though it tarries, wait for it, because it will surely come, it will not tarry."*

Sometimes we simply do not understand the things that God asks of us and we can make the mistake of trying to work things out when we just need to walk out where we are. There is a beautiful simplicity in accepting God's prophetic word and just living day by day. If the desire of your heart is to be a man or woman of strategy in God's kingdom, then you need to be living in that place of conversation with God. Can I challenge you? When was the last time you had a conversation with God? When did you last simply sit with him, invite him to talk to you? I'm not talking about a Bible study or a prayer meeting, but heart-to-heart time. We are living in a time when we need our conversations with heaven to change situations on earth.

2.   *Joshua claimed his inheritance.*

In accordance with the strategy that God had given Joshua, we see Joshua and the Israelites march round the walls of Jericho—not your average battle plan. Why did God have them walk round the walls? It wasn't just because they needed the exercise! I believe that this was a spiritual declaration to the ground that they were about to conquer; it was a statement to the principalities and powers that God was about to move. Jericho was a city that engaged in Baal worship and practises detestable to the people of God and everything was about to change. Marching round the city was a declaration that things were about to change, that this was God's ground.

Go back with me to Genesis 13: 17 where God promises Abram that wherever he puts his foot will be his. From the beginning of time, creation has known it has to respond to the plans and purposes of heaven. Look at creation itself— creation responds to the voice of the creator. There was no way anyone could oppose Abram when, wherever he stood was declared his by the creator, there was no way those walls of Jericho could physically hold when the voice of the creator spoke to the very foundations on which they hand been built. Claiming your inheritance isn't just about words that sound good but an intrinsic belief that God will give you that which he has set aside for you. I believe that with every step Abram took there was a heart that said, '*Thank you for this land*,' I believe that with every step Joshua took there was an excitement that waited to see what Gods would do. Something I really think is important is prayer walking. I am passionate for my nation, England, for it to remember its powerful heritage and live in it. We need to learn to remind the ground that we stand on is holy ground.

Something I used to do to when I was a secondary school teacher was pray in my classrooms before the pupils arrived, particularly for the more troublesome classes! As I spoke over my classrooms it reminded my spirit that God was in this space and that because God was in this space it was anointed space, holy space and holy ground. The order of heaven had to transcend the order of earth! I remember the apostle to our group of churches, Keri Jones, sharing a conversation he had had with a car salesman and Keri had turned round and said, '*Do you know who I am?*' The car salesman looked somewhat confused, and I can't quite remember the gist of the response but it was about being the son of a king, I think! When we know who we are and what we stand on our eyes are opened to see so much more. It is time to march round your inheritance again.

3.   Joshua made sure the ark was in its proper place.

When you look at the order in Joshua 6, you see that this march round Jericho had a position and a place for everyone. There is the armed guard first, and then the priests blowing trumpets, then the ark, and then the rear guard, this is no scrum but an ordered procession. I find the position of the ark of the Lord really interesting. It is between the guards in the middle of the battle. It is after the noise, after the battle cry, and it is before the people. In Old Testament times the ark was symbolic of the presence of God. It contained the laws of God inside it. In our lives and in our battles where is the presence of God? Where are the laws of God? There would have been no point in the ark going out if the people weren't living by the laws it contained. You cannot expect God to bless you if you live in disobedience. The ark going first means two things, 1) it means that we inhabit the presence of God and 2) that we live in obedience to him. How do we inhabit the presence of God? There was a phrase banded about in Christian circles a while ago—you may remember it? *Practise the Presence*, it was known as. In other words, cultivating time to be with God and to hear God, learning to listen in the little things,—who do you want me to talk to in this room? And in the bigger things, seeking God for direction for the future. Living in the presence of God needs to be a habit not a hobby. If we aren't careful we can be awesome about having hobbies and awful at cultivating habits.

The best way I have found in practising the presence of God is to look at the everyday. For example, on a Saturday morning I do housework; a part of my well-ordered routine! I have made it my practise to pray as I clean the bathroom and run the hover round. When I used to commute to work, I would make it my practise to pray when driving to work in the mornings, to pour out the day before God before it got started. When you practise the presence of heaven, heaven's solutions begin to manifest more and more in your life— they have to because in conversation, earth and heaven are lining up.

As we learn what it means to dwell in the presence of God, God highlights things in our lives that need changing. He shows us how to live in obedience. The things God highlights are designed to draw us into further intimacy, not to convince us to run as fast as possible in the other direction. God is a God of exchange. When He highlights something in our lives it is in order that He can take it and give us something better. When we understand God's heart for exchange, it changes our view of obedience, that it isn't '*do this or else,*' but '*do this because.*' Because Joshua walked in total obedience to the strategy of heaven, not a life of Joshua's army was lost in the 'Battle of Jericho,' no one was injured. They simply observed the hand of God. Outside of obedience there is grace but there is also tremendous cost. For Abraham, the cost of meddling with God's strategy meant that he had to abandon his first-born son (Ishmael). The grace of God covers us, and

I know that I can look at my own life and see that on many levels! But the obedience to God protects us—the blessings of obedience are not something we fully realise this side of heaven. We can't see what the consequences would have been, but we know that in every choice we make that submits to the will of God there is blessing. Do we need to learn again what it means to dwell in his presence and not simply dash in and out when we have time?

4.   Joshua knew the power of the noise and the silence of heaven.

I don't know what kind of person you are, whether you are someone who loves to be in a place of high praise, shouting, singing, dancing, etc., or whether you are someone who likes the more intimate times of worship, the quieter songs that linger in His presence. I love the quiet worship, the gentle stillness, and just lingering in the presence of God. I have to admit I am not a huge fan of loud praise, but I am learning and realising more and more that you can't have one without the other! God wants his people to understand both the noise and the silence of heaven. I find Joshua 6 really interesting. The people walk in a place of silence for six days, not a word and not a sound as they march, but then, when they are given a word to shout, they shout in unison and the walls fall. We need to be a people who understand the silence and the shout. You can't carry on a conversation with two people talking over each other, one has to listen. If we want heaven to speak, we have to listen. That means we have to be silent. Nowhere in the Bible does it talk of having a prayer for every situation, sometimes we can be too good at words. The Bible does speak of groans that words cannot express—Romans 8: 26—of allowing the spirit to make intercessions for us. In our worship we must make sure that we allow room for the quietness of heaven. It is the quietness that prepares the shout. When the Israelites came to shout they had six days worth of praise that was just ready to come forth. They knew exactly the right words to shout, because they had spent six days seeking God for them and they were prepared to make a noise!

Just as the silence of heaven is a powerful thing, so the noise of heaven is a powerful thing. At Pentecost, the Holy Spirit is described as a mighty rushing wind (Acts 2: 2); it invaded the house where they all were and turned the situation on its head! Notice however that before the noise there was unity, in Joshua 6 the people all shouted together, in Acts they were all *'with one accord, in one place'* (Acts 2: 1). This was not random noise; this was a piercing from heaven to earth. If you just make noise, you will just hear noise because God will not bless chaos. A united noise, a shout of praise from God's people, declaring his goodness—now that is a different thing! Heaven changes earth and walls fall down. I have been in meetings where we have sung high praise songs and I haven't felt like singing them. I haven't wanted to sing them, but I have because I recognise the power of joining with God's people to declare his praise. In singing those songs, I am declaring that the noise of heaven will change my situation. Sometimes you just need to get over yourself and shout (I speak from experience), sometimes you just need to get over yourself and listen (I'm still speaking from experience!). If we just live in the beauty of the silence of heaven, we will never declare the wonders of God. We won't see his purposes burst forth. If we just live in the noise of heaven, we become clanging cymbals. We need to learn to discern the time for silence and the time for noise and not despise either one. To despise the silence of God is to despise the answer, to despise the noise of heaven is to despise the outworking of the answer—you can't have one without the other. Ecclesiastes talks about a time for silence and a time to speak (Ecclesiastes 3: 7), when was the last time we were silent? When was the last time we shouted with everything within us? Sometimes when our flesh screams at the very thought of shouting or of the gentle conversation, that is actually a good indicator that that is what we should be doing!

5.   Joshua knew the strategy for handling the victory.

In every strategy of heaven there is a victory, after all. God doesn't set us up to lose. For the Israelites, that meant burning Jericho and taking only a few things to be used in the service of the temple. It would have been very easy, in all the excitement, to maybe take a few things and to pretend that it didn't really matter; Achan did this and paid the price. How we handle victory is very important because it leads us into the next battle. If we handle victory wrongly, we set ourselves up to fail—this is what would happen in Joshua 7. How do we handle the victory that God gives us? Joshua understood the need to destroy what had just been captured For the Israelites, that battle was part of a journey, not a place to settle. We need to know what our victory means, what we learn from each battle, what we take with us, and what we leave behind. We can be very good at asking for heaven's strategies to get us out of the pit, but what about the strategies for the good times, for the next level? Heaven's strategies are not restricted to things that are awful, there is a completeness of the strategy of heaven that sets us up for the future. If we want to see more of heaven on earth we need to make sure we know the strategy for the victory.

I was watching a film about figure-skating and one of the comments made was that your last move should lead into your next one. The same principle applies in God. We need to be a people leaning into the next thing God has for us— the strategy for victory!

6.   And for Rahab.

I couldn't let this chapter go by without recognizing the amazing bravery of this woman. Because of Rahab's actions, all her family were saved; the only ones to survive Jericho from the inside. Joshua's strategy and her own obedience saved her life and her relatives—something they did not fully appreciate until they saw the devastation from the outside. The fact that they survived was a miracle, and they survived to worship a God who had saved their lives (and destroyed every God they would have worshipped before!). There was total confidence in the part of the spies that in the miracle God would protect Rahab. Logistically it seemed impossible. After all a red chord from a window wouldn't be much in an earthquake, but God saw. Sometimes we can't see how the strategy of heaven works out, we just need to give away what God has given us and know that, in our obedience, God extends his protection over our households. As we live in his presence and learn to move in the plans and purposes of heaven, God covers us and those close to us.

Just as Joshua understood and walked out the strategy that God gave him, we need to be a people that look to the strategy of heaven in order to see God's kingdom come on earth.

CHAPTER 11

A Man Who Got It Wrong Sometimes

In Joshua Chapter 7, we see Joshua get it wrong in a big way. Up until now he has acted with a maturity and integrity that set him apart from the rest of his people. He is a man whom God has used to do mighty miracles, he has seen awesome things. He is just beginning to get a proper handle on leadership, and then this, the death of thirty-six men in a battle that they should have won easily. It must have seemed to Joshua that his world was turning on his head again, how could he ever get it back? Yet Joshua didn't allow his place of defeat to be the end of the journey; it became a place that he never came back to.

God knows that we will get it wrong sometimes, the greatest pressure to be better, achieve, more often comes from ourselves. Joshua lived through his mistake. He had to face the same battle again in Joshua 8; he didn't run away, he didn't give up, and he dealt with the consequences that his leadership had caused. In his grace God wove the disobedience of the Israelites and Joshua into a victory on his tapestry (Joshua 8). What can we learn from the man who got it wrong sometimes? How can we be a people who live in the freedom from our mistakes and not the condemnation of them?

1. The place of good ideas and advice versus the place of godly counsel.

It must have seemed like a good idea to send spies up from Jericho to Ai (Joshua 7:2), it seemed a sensible recommendation that only a few thousand men marched up to Ai (Joshua

7: 3). None of these things are appalling suggestions. They seem to make sense, but what lets them down is the absence of heaven's input. We need to be a people who listen to the counsel of God first, who search out his wisdom. We can be very wise sometimes at sending mavericks packing and dismissing lunatic ideas but miss the danger of 'good advice.' Why devise a cunning plan when God can give you a perfect plan? Well meaning people can do incredible damage. To know where you are going you need to understand the heart of God, not the opinions and suggestions of everyone around you. We need to go to God for our plan first and then look to our wise counsel for input. Joshua never set out to be deliberately disobedient, he just got carried away. They had just won an awesome victory, he knew how it could work this time, he saw no reason why it shouldn't, so he just went ahead. There is no mention of asking God anywhere, he had forgotten that the voice of God is the authority.

We cannot move and expect God to bless whatever we choose to do. If we want heaven's answer and heaven's strategy, we need to align ourselves with heaven. Heaven won't give in and let earth have the miracle its own way. The walls fell because the whole army was together; the foundations had no choice but to crumble. You can't expect mountains to move when you stand in disobedience; the treasure buried in the ground was like a physical barrier that separated the Israelites from the covering of their Lord. We cannot blame God when our good ideas land us in trouble and we have taken ourselves out from under his covering; it is time to be a people who walk in the place of obedience.

2.   The place of disobedience: defeat and desolation

In Joshua 7: 8 we hear the heart of a desperate man *"Ah, Sovereign Lord, why did you ever bring this people across the Jordan to deliver us into the hands of the Amorites to destroy us."* Joshua has gone from the confidence of the miracle to the doubt that they were even right to cross the Jordan. Notice how his one mistake is magnified until it throws up doubts like *'all my decisions are wrong, everything is about to go wrong, this is all a nightmare.'* [My paraphrase of Verses 6–9]. When mistakes dominate our life and our confession, they will make us doubt the promises and the plans of God. I am sure that Joshua felt crushed after the blood of thirty-six men was on his head. Joshua knew what it was like to feel desolate and alone, but he didn't stay in a place of desolation. What happens when we make a mistake? For Joshua, his mistake cost lives, but he didn't resign as general however much he may have wanted to. Did you know that God inhabits the place of desolation with the answer that brings us up out of the pit? The place of desolation is the place where we cast ourselves back on God again, the place where we repent of our mistakes and realign ourselves with heaven's plan. In Psalm 51 we read of David's despair as he repents of his adultery, he realises how much his sin has hurt God and the mess he has created, in intercession he pleads with God, *"Do not cast me from your presence or take your holy spirit from me. Restore to me the joy of your salvation and grant me a willing spirit to sustain me. Then I will teach transgressors your ways and sinners will turn back to you"* (Psalm 51:11–13). David recognises that it isn't just about giving up but being restored back to a place where he is fulfilling God's plan over his life.

If we allow mistakes to dictate our position, we will end up in a place of condemnation, outside of the things God has for us. God is a transforming God; he wants to turn our mistakes into something beautiful. Joshua's mistake became another victory, we need to live in this principle, and our mistakes should become another victory.

It seems very easy to say this and I can almost hear the response *'you don't know the horror of my mistakes.'* God understands the awfulness of our darkest moment, but there is no mistake that cannot become a victory and no defeat that cannot be transformed. We start in the place of repentance, the place that Joshua went to when he fell face down before the ark of God; we come into the presence of God.

3.   *The place of absolute, the place of holiness*

God's response to Joshua almost seems quite harsh, *"Stand up! What are you doing down on your face? Israel has sinned they have violated my covenant."* (Joshua 7: 10–11). You can almost imagine God speaking to Joshua *'enough now, it's time to sort this out.'* God is the God of absolutes, when he tells us not to do something it is a matter of importance whether we choose to obey or not. There is power in the obedience of God's people; the Israelites had just seen that when, with one shout, the walls fell down. We can make the mistake sometimes of treating God like an indulgent grandparent, thinking he will just turn a blind eye as we do things we shouldn't do just one more time. Such a view of God is a misunderstanding of his character; God is a holy God, so holy that when Jesus was on the cross—wearing our sin—God had to turn his face away. When we ask to live in a place of miracle power, we are living in a place where our obedience is of paramount importance. I remember watching a video about a revival in Latin America that was taking place. A pastor was sharing about the amazing sense of the holiness of God that had everyone on their knees as the sound desk shook, he remembered knowing *'one wrong move and your dead!'*

Is God going round with some kind of zapper gun, looking at us when we aren't 100 percent on form? No, but we need to understand something more of the holiness of God. As we align ourselves with heaven, things on earth move in obedient and things in the heavenly battle change. We are operating with our eyes on a different level, we see miracles, we see healings, and we see salvation with signs and wonders following. What we can't then do is apply the earthy principles we have abandoned for our benefit, such an act makes a mockery of the provision of God, because the holiness of God confronts the lie. Think of it like this, in the place of miracles, God's holiness, his sovereignty confronts a situation and turns it on its head. That situation is transformed to reflect the holiness of God. The same applies in reverse. When you confront God's holiness with rebellion, lying, greed etc., God will turn that situation to reflect his holiness—it is the same thing.

After God has spoken to Joshua and told him what has happened, God instructs the Israelites to have a time of consecration, they need time to remember who God is. God was very clear, *"you cannot stand against your enemies until you remove it [that which has been stolen]"* Joshua 7: 13. The Israelites have got to sort out this mistake before they can move on. It is no good repenting and spending time in intercession if the loot stays under the ground, God is very clear, they won't win anymore battles until they sort it out. Sometimes there are blockages in our lives that we need to deal with; we can repent of the same thing over and over again without actually removing the blockage. Our repentance and our actions need to go hand in hand; otherwise, we will end up in a place of frustration or hypocrisy. God was very clear with Joshua what the problem was and will search our hearts if we ask him; maybe it's time to do some digging!

4.   The place of treasure

For Achan his place of treasure was in things, in stability, in the chance to own things he had always wanted, his treasure was in an easy inheritance, not the inheritance he had journeyed for. Jesus said, *"For where your treasure is, there your heart will be also."* (Luke 12: 34). Joshua had spent a life cultivating treasures that were nothing to do with material possessions. He had cultivated a spirit of worship, a heart for prayer and intercession, discernment, and he had spent his years in the wilderness cultivating something that was irreplaceable. Achan, on the other hand (I believe), had spent his desert time wanting and waiting for the chance to have some land—to have some 'things.' Everything we own is a blessing from God. We don't own anything that he didn't give us, and we moan sometimes that we haven't got enough. It is a sobering question to ask yourself, *'where is my heart?'* A heart after God places its treasure in an inheritance that it can't always see, but an inheritance that it trusts for. 1 Peter 1: 3–4 states, *"Praise be to the God and Father of our Lord Jesus Christ! In his great mercy he has given us new birth into a living hope, through the resurrection of the dead, and into an inheritance that can never spoil or fade—kept in heaven for you."* That is where our treasure is. It is easy to look to your inheritance in good times, but what about in barren times, in desert times? Where is your treasure when things are awful? Sometimes it is in the awfulness of life that the inheritance of treasure in heaven grows; treasure that has been refined by fire and fought for with determination.

5.   *The place of fire*

The end of this chapter sees a bloodbath as Achan and all his family and livestock are stoned to death and then burned—a grim ending. I wonder what it cost Israel to stone him? How did Achan's relatives feel about killing him? It can't have been a pleasant experience. Here isn't the place to dwell on the why of the stoning. I will leave that for someone else's book! In the end, Achan left an inheritance that was a valley called Achor, or trouble. In attempting to shore up a wrong inheritance, he and his family lost his inheritance. We need to be honest before God. God isn't fooled by our hypocrisy, we can be very good at kidding other people, even kidding ourselves, but God knows where we are. We can be very judgemental of Achan for his actions, but many of us do similar things, we bury our desires, our treasures away and fail to grasp the heart of God that we release those things to be given so much more. It is time to be vulnerable again before God, to allow him to search our tents, our wallets, and our hearts.

6.   The place of victory

Joshua 8: Contrast for a moment the attitude of Joshua and the attitude of Achan to their mistakes. Joshua repents; he goes to the presence of God and looks for the answer of God. Achan only confesses to his mistake when forced to do so. Joshua went on to win the next battle (the same one he had just lost) but Achan died. God sees our mistakes and our failures; he wants us to be vulnerable with him, to come back to him again for heaven's answer, heaven's way forward. God doesn't call us to be a people who bury our mistakes, who live in hypocrisy, or who think they don't matter,—living like this is contrary to the will of God. When we understand more of the forgiveness of God, we learn to deal with our mistakes and move on. We realize that God is in our vulnerability and our heart to get it right, and that in our treasure he is preparing our inheritance.

David wrote *"Cleanse me with hyssop and I shall be clean, wash me and I shall be whiter than snow, let the bones you have crushed rejoice. Hide your face from my sin and blot out my iniquity."* Psalm 51: 7–9. David was a man who knew what it was like to mess up, but also who knew how to receive the forgiveness of God. It is time to be a people who leave our mistakes behind and learn what it means to live more and more in the grace of God.

CHAPTER 12

A Man Who Had to
Deal with Deception

Sometimes we can be caught out because we stay in a place of complacency. The Israelites have just destroyed Ai and renewed their Covenant with God, the words of the law are fresh in their minds and the joy of the victory they have just experienced gives anticipation and excitement. Because they are so elated by what has just happened, they are not prepared for the delegation of Gibeonite's who appear and, in consequence, end up in a place of disobedience. It is good to live in the victory but our eyes must remain on the victor, victory isn't just a place of celebration but of growth—a place of communion with God where we learn more about him and where we experience a deeper level of relationship.

1 Peter 5: 8 talks about the enemy as a roaring lion, prowling round—as Christians we need to be alert and ready, never deserting our place as watchmen so that when attack comes we meet it and chase it away before it has the chance to become a battle. Habakkuk 2: 1 reveals the heart of the prophet when he writes *"I will stand at my watch and station myself on the ramparts; I will look and see what he will say to me, and what answer I am to give to this complaint."* The following verses give God's answer, containing amazing promises.

We can be very good sometimes at living in communion with God in the anguish of the battle, of walking side by side with him through the carnage of the battlefield and the barrage of attack, but what happens to that communion in the victory? We must not allow the place of communion to give way to the place of complacency.

Let us look at the Gibeonite deception and learn from both Joshua's mistakes and his wisdom.

1.   *They had heard the rumours.*

The Gibeonite's were not daft! They knew the Israelites by reputation (Joshua 9: 24). They even knew the prophetic word—their days were numbered. They were wise enough not to join in the war that the other kings proposed (Joshua 9:2) as they knew they would lose, instead, they resort to an elaborate ploy. The rumours that had spread were sufficient to enable the Gibeonites to a) recognise the supremacy of God, b) understand what the prophetic word meant for them, and c) devise a cunning plan. I wonder what would have happened if they would have just stuck with a and b? The rumours of the exploits of the people of God were enough for the sovereignty of God to be recognised and taken seriously. What do people say about us? What are the rumours that go round about us? Do people look at our churches and say, *'Have you heard what happens there? Do you know people are healed there? Situations change there when they pray!'* The people of God should be people with a reputation that goes before them. The Biblical precedent is that we preach the word and there are signs and wonders following—just look at the life and ministry of Jesus, you can't have one without the other. If you want to see miracles, look to the preaching of the word—the two go hand in hand.

For the Israelites, it all went wrong with the Gibeonites when they accepted their story. Note that we are not responsible with dealing with the fallout of rumours—that is not our calling. Every story, every 'truth' must check out against the truth of the word of God. We do not need to 'deal' God out of trouble we simply stand in the identity that created the rumour!

2.   *It all seemed very genuine.*

One of the things that struck me about the Gibeonites was how they seemed so very genuine to the Israelites. The Gibeonites had thought out their plan well, and it was a good plan—it worked! We need to be careful of things that seem genuine and that seem good, but are actually distractions, lies, and plans contrary to the purposes of God. Truth is not truth until it lines up against God's plumb line of truth. The Israelites fell down because they checked out the truth practically (they sampled their bread), they had the mentality of, *'this seems okay to us,'* but they didn't seek God. Often the most dangerous things are not things that are obviously bad but things that appear good but are really dangerous, just look at Genesis 3. In Genesis 3, the serpent convinces Eve that God is a liar—you can almost hear him wheedling away, sounding like he only has Eve's best interests at heart! As a result of listening to the serpent, Eve ends up living her life under a curse. In 2 Corinthians 11: 1–15, Paul writes to the Corinthian church about false apostles masquerading as the real thing. These apostles appeared like the genuine article to the Corinthian church and, because the Corinthian Church liked what they heard, they became convinced that these apostles were the real thing; these false apostles knew what to say but their life style didn't match up. We need to be a people who walk in discernment and who know how to weigh and test things in the spirit. Becoming a people of discernment means living a lifestyle of discernment, and checking with God at every opportunity. The more that we seek to discern the will of God, the more we will find ourselves in his perfect will.

3.   *It all went wrong when they left God out.*

"The men of Israel sampled their provisions but did not enquire of the Lord." (Joshua 9: 14). I wonder what would have happened if they had stopped to check it out? Hindsight is a

wonderful thing and 'if only' is a question we often ask ourselves. Israel's history shows a pattern, when they walk with
God they live in victory and win their battles, when they turn
away, disaster happens and stays until they repent. Hear me
right; to live in victory means you have to fight battles, you
can't win without advancing. When we ask God to inhabit
our decisions, we invite the victory of heaven to move on
earth. You can't expect heaven's order, its miracle-working
power, and it's angelic presence to manifest itself if you live
your circumstances under your own agenda. I really aspire to
be like Deborah, who lived her life listening to the agenda of
heaven. We read Deborah's story in Judges 4 and 5, she [Deb-
orah] receives a word from God and sends for the army commander, she tells him to ride out against an opposing army
and there will be victory. The army commander [Barak] has
no mind to go anywhere; he had not been listening for a word
and is not keen to ride into what he perceives will be disaster;
he will only go if she goes with him! Deborah agrees to go at
once, so certain is she of her word that she knows the victory
is already there. We fight battles every day, but the outcome
of the war is already determined, the script isn't wrong and
it cannot be changed. If we can get into the habit of allowing
God to pierce our agenda's, we lose the fallout in creating
our own agenda's. I love The Message version of Corinthians
where it says, '*Let the word of Christ— The Message—Have
the run of the house.*'[26] Imagine the difference if God's word
was given free reign—it is time to be a people who walk with
increased discernment.

4.   *The integrity of Joshua*

One thing that really struck me about this chapter was the
integrity of Joshua in it all, it would be very easy for him
to be exceedingly angry . After all, he had just been tricked
and manipulated. Not only that but (possibly predictably) the

---

[26]Colossians 3: 14–16

Israelites were blaming him and the other leaders. The first thing that we notice is that Joshua honours his oath before God, even though he knew he was wrong to have made it. There are consequences to our actions and sometimes we need to learn how to live in the consequences of wrong actions. Joshua could have justifiably said that the oath didn't stand because it was made under false pretences, he could have manipulated the situation to make himself look good again. In recognising the oath, Joshua is recognising that he cannot go back on what he has promised before God, in doing 'nothing,' he is leaving the situation with God, the answer is God's responsibility. I know that when I make a mistake my instinct is to run around and sort it out as quick as I can before I have to admit to anyone that I am wrong and let them deal with the fallout. Often, when I do this, I can make things worse. Sometimes we compound our mistakes by trying to fix them; thinking then they will appear 'better' before God. God desires first our genuine repentance; it is only then that we receive his strategy for moving forward.

Notice that the Gibeonites reap their own punishment for their deception, not only do they end up living under a curse but they end up living under the position of God (Joshua 9: 23 and 27). What does it mean to live like that? I wonder if the Gibeonites realized in all of this that their clever scam was actually not that great.

In it all there is a challenge of integrity to us. How do we deal with people who deceive us, who enter our lives under 'false pretences' and bring false promises? Notice the reaction of the people compared to the reaction of Joshua, the Israelite people are all for apportioning blame (Joshua 9: 18–19) but Joshua is looking for heaven's answer. It is very easy sometimes to apportion blame, *'They told me he/she was alright'* or *'I wouldn't have done it on my own but they convinced me.'* Apportioning blame will only bring you to a standstill; whereas looking for heaven's answer moves you forward. God sees those people who have wrecked havoc on our lives and part of heaven's answer is allowing God to deal with them, only then can we move forward effectively. The Gibeonites didn't get away with their trickery. They suffered an awful punishment—what must it be like to live your life under a curse? When we allow God the role of avenger we let go of the headspace that disappointment and disillusionment cost us, we invite heaven's answer into our own lives. Deuteronomy 32: 35 states, "Vengeance is Mine and recompense." (NKJ Version).

God wants a people who live in integrity. A people who live in integrity make a powerful statement to the world around them. The Gibeonites knew Joshua was a man of integrity and they took advantage knowing that he couldn't go back on his oath. What they hadn't reckoned on was God seeing. We don't need to try to do God's work for him; we need to live in the calling that he has set before us.

5.   The Israelites had to come back to the position of God.

I find it really interesting that, at the end of Chapter 9, we are back in the position of God. Reading on to Chapter 10, we see the conversation again between God and Joshua. The heart of God is in relationship with his people, in moving on with them. Joshua is never identified as 'the man who was deceived' or even as 'the man who learned from his mistakes.' He dealt with these situations and moved on. We can learn from the example of Joshua in how we deal with our mistakes, mistakes are never meant to become our identity but we can let them define us if we aren't careful.

Let me share an illustration with you. I have a puppet parrot called Percy who squawks when he speaks. He comes with me into primary schools and plays the flashcard game (a game that I use to help children remember key vocabulary). Generally, we play the pupils against Percy and Percy always loses, he can't help choosing the wrong flashcard, even when thirty children are screaming at him, 'noooo Percy,' he still manages to pick the wrong one—he never listens, but his heart is in the right place! But the children love Percy, and they are so eager for him to get it right that they want him to go again and again. They all want to hold him, stroke him, ask him questions, they love him. God is like that with us, even when we get it wrong and we have all of heaven screaming at us 'Don't do it, stop, that's not clever!' he just wants us to come back to him and move on.

There is always hope when we come back to the perfect position of heaven. The enemy would have us believe that mistakes paralyze us, this is a lie. And too often a very effective one. We need to be like Joshua in holding lightly to our mistakes, in dealing quickly and moving on. Identifying with the psalmist:

> *"All my enemies whisper together against me; they imagine the worst for me saying, 'a vile disease has beset him, he will never get up from the place where he lies,' even my close friend, whom I trusted, he who shared his bread, has lifted up his heel against me."* (Psalm 41: 7–9)

and confessing:

> *"But you, O Lord, have mercy upon me; raise me up, that I may repay them. I know that you are pleased with me, for my enemy does not triumph over me. In my integrity you uphold me and set me in your presence forever. Praise be to the Lord, the God of Israel, from everlasting to everlasting."* (Psalm 41: 10–13)

CHAPTER 13

A Man Who Understood His Authority

"I have given you authority to trample on snakes and scorpions and to overcome all the power of the enemy; nothing will harm you. However, do not rejoice that the spirits submit to you, but rejoice that your names are written in heaven."

Luke 10: 19–20

Joshua's walk was a walk marked out with authority. This was a man who knew the power of communion with heaven and who watched heaven change earth's circumstances. Joshua was also a man who walked with great integrity and who honoured the promises he had made before God. He understood the fact that God transforms our mistakes and he watched his army and heavens army battle together.

In our nation we need to get back to that place of authority that is covered by our integrity. What does it do when we command time to stand still? Too often we are guilty of moaning that there aren't enough hours in the day—what would happen if the appointments of each day belonged to God? What would happen if we caught the prophetic word? If we understood the place of intercession that causes the sun to stand still? The sun doesn't stand still to allow us to accomplish our agenda, it stands still for the purpose and promise of heaven to affect earth—we need to know what we are asking for.

As we look at Joshua 10, we see a man of tremendous authority—to command the sun and the moon you have to be used to moving from a heavenly perspective. The fact that the sun and the moon recognised the voice of authority indicates that creation itself knew what it was dealing with. We can stand and shout at creation all we like but outside of the authority of God and the anointing of heaven creation doesn't move. What can we learn from Joshua's example? How do we operate in the authority that God has given us?

Let us look at seven principles that can help us:

1.   The place of authority is a lifestyle of integrity.

Are you the real deal? The place of authority is a place of absolute; it is not a grey area. James 5: 12 talks about our yes being yes and our no being no. If you want to move in authority you need to live a life of integrity. To live a life of integrity is to line your life up with the word of God. When we live lives under the order of heaven, creation has to move itself to line up with heavens order and circumstances have to change to line up with heaven's plans. Acts 19 talks about Paul's ministry in Ephesus, how he saw people healed, baptized in the spirit, etc. Some of the Jews saw what Paul was doing and decided they would have a go and tried driving out evil spirits themselves, they got a shock when the evil spirit turned round and answered them, saying, *"Jesus I know, and I know about Paul, but who are you?"*[27] The heavenly realm saw what was happening in Paul's ministry, they recognised a man of authority. Living in integrity and authority didn't mean Paul had an easy life. Paul's integrity meant he suffered beatings and false imprisonment, it meant that he worshipped in prison when he probably didn't feel like it. Integrity isn't simply about living a 'good' life; it is about making God choices. Let me give you a practical example, when I worked as a youth worker I was determined I would not just read the Bible for preparing youth sessions or talks. Before I

---

[27]Acts 19: 11–16

came to do any preparation, I would make sure I had my own time in the word. I live now in the blessing of that integrity, I write out of the wealth that I learned then.

For Joshua, walking in integrity meant that he honoured the oath he had made towards the Gibeonites, even though he knew he had been wrong to make the oath in the first place. There is an important principle of integrity here, in honouring this oath. Joshua is not glossing over his mistake, nor is he making his mistake worse, he is trusting God with the fallout of his mistake. We can trust God with the fallout of our mistakes; Joshua knew the Israelites now had a duty of responsibility towards the Gibeonites, even though that was never the way it was intended. In walking in integrity, Joshua presents God with an opportunity to move mightily. Even in our mistakes we should never lose our integrity, if we can stand in our mistakes in integrity we allow the transforming power of God to work a miracle. In Joshua's integrity there comes a prophetic word (Joshua 10: 8) and an amazing victory. What looked like a rescue mission became an awesome display of the power of God.

2.   In the place of authority the resources of heaven override the natural.

When Joshua told his army that they were to march through the night to rescue the Gibeonites, I suspect he wasn't very popular. The Gibeonites were probably not the Israelites favourite people and the prospect of marching through the night not something the Israelite army relished. I imagine the grumbles against Joshua the comments of, *'how does he expect us to fight now when we're all exhausted?'* etc. I also imagine the surprise when the army starts to fight and finds the opposing army in chaos, I bet the Israelites didn't even feel tired! When we walk in our authority, the resources of heaven override the situations that we find ourselves in. In Judges 7, we read the story of Gideon. This was a man who had all his 'natural' resources stripped away and found himself in a place of relying on supernatural interference, as he rose up in his leadership he found the resources of heaven moving for him.

Sometimes God allows our resources to be stripped away Then, in the victory, we recognise heaven's hand. I remember being in a meeting and playing in the worship team, a prophetic word was brought and one of the leaders of the meeting caught my attention and said, *'play your flute.'* I panicked as I had been playing my saxophone up until that point and knew that my flute would sound awful as I had no time to warm up or adjust. In obedience, I picked up my flute and played out, wincing as I heard the tone of the first few notes, but then, God took it and what came out was anointed playing and God moved. When we allow God to stretch us, when we respond to authority with authority, we are operating in a powerful place. When nothing in us wants to move, it is then that everything in us has to give over to the agenda of heaven.

3.   Standing in the place of authority we see God fights for us.

Reading Joshua 10, I just have this amazing picture in my head of God hurling hailstones down on a retreating, battered, and very scared opposing army; it must have been an awesome sight to see. I imagine Joshua looking and surveying the scene, thinking to himself, *'So that's how He was going to do it!'* Are we looking to see the hailstones from heaven? When we stand in authority there is a place of seeing, of standing with a confidence that knows heaven is ready to move. We need to be a people who expect the interference of heaven in our lives.

The story in 1 Samuel 19: 18–24 always makes me laugh. Saul is in pursuit of David and sends men to capture him; however, David is with Samuel prophesying and all that happens to Saul's army is that each group of men come back without David and prophesying. Eventually, in disgust, Saul goes himself and ends up coming back prophesying, without David,—he got more than he bargained for! Notice, David doesn't seem worried by all of this, he knows he is where he should be and, standing with the prophet of God, he simply watches and enjoys heavens interference. The place of authority isn't necessarily a very easy place but there is peace for us in the place of authority, there is space to see heaven fight for us. Do we need to look again for the hailstone in heaven?

4.   God calls us to know the authority that we possess.

The one thing that really stands out to me about Joshua was that here was a man who knew his authority. After all, if he had announced *'moon stand still'* and nothing had happened, he would have looked pretty stupid. Joshua had such a heart for the plans and purposes of God that he recognised that the Israelites needed more time to win the battle; he wanted to complete the job God had given him. Here was a man with such a heart for God that he stopped time. Do we know the authority that we carry? Do we really realise the power than we have? Knowing the authority we posses enables us to stand when things are awful. Paul writes to the church as Colossi, *'Set your minds on things above, not on earthly things.'*[28] In other words, *'know who you are and know who is on your side.'* When we know the authority we possess we can take it to our neighbourhoods, to our workplaces, to our families. Wherever Jesus was people were healed, he could help himself, in his love and mercy he reached out. Through Jesus death and resurrection we have that same authority.

Knowing our authority does not mean we shout at every created thing. If you want creation to move, you have to be prepared for an all night march. We are good sometimes at trying to command things to bend to our will and not

---

[28]Colossians 3: 2

spending time in preparation first. We can pray *'Lord, send revival'* and sometimes I imagine God saying to us in response, *'What would you do if I did?'* If we are serious about revival in our nation, we need to be a people of intercession, we need to search out the heart of God and walk in integrity in his word. Joshua's shout came out of a place that knew the prophetic word, that walked the edge, and that had already seen awesome things. It came out of a place of expectation but more than anything else, it came out of a cry and a desire for the completeness of God's hand. How much do we really want what God has for us?

5.   *Authority rolls away stones.*

When we operate in the authority God has for us, we become good at recognizing times and seasons. In Joshua 10: 16–21, we see Joshua command the leaders of the army to be shut in a cave, they are a distraction to be dealt with later. When we operate in authority we fight the right battles, sometimes we can wonder what is going on, maybe we are fighting the wrong battle, maybe we have been distracted. Joshua recognizes God's timing and God's battle plan. At the right time God will always roll away the stone, just look at Lazarus or look at the resurrection. People thought God had got it wrong, left it too late. What they had misunderstood was what God had said. They didn't realise that God was waiting for the perfect time. God is the God of ultimate victory, and his victory is always victory at the right time.

6.   *In your authority stand in your victory.*

Look for a moment at Joshua 10: 21–26 and consider Joshua's actions. Why did he do what he did? For me, I see Joshua leaving an example—a heritage. The commanders of the army would have been at least forty years his junior, they would have out-lived him He was leaving them something to remember, he was depositing a principle into their lives that they would never forget, this was a moment of teaching *'this is who you are, this is where your enemies live.'* Those men would never forget standing on the necks of those kings, he was leaving them a reminder, remember what God did, remember that nothing can stand against him, remember that there is nothing that God can't do. Joshua was showing his army how to stand in their victory; it had to be a complete victory. Look at the prophetic word in Verse 25. Joshua knew that God was going to give the Israelites more victory. Standing on the necks of those kings sent a message to the supernatural realm, *'these battles are won'*—standing on the necks of those kings made a mockery of the enemy's schemes. It was a powerful declaration, *'nothing can stand against us.'* What an awesome legacy. How do we stand in our victory? What are we teaching in the legacy we leave?

Just before Jesus died he let rip with a shout of triumph,[29] the fight was over, a lamb had defeated the serpent. At that moment in time, it didn't look like a shout of victory, it seemed like just the opposite, but in reality things the power of death was broken, broken in such a way that tombs themselves came open.[30] No one who witnessed what had happened would ever be the same again.

That which is dead comes alive by a word from God—just look at Ezekiel 37. It is time to be that prophetic voice which speaks life into dead situations, which sees the victory of God. When we see in the spirit, we see the victory before it is even there. In 1 Kings 18: 41–46, Elijah heard the rain. He knew it was coming before it was even on the horizon. He made his servant check again and again because he knew what he had heard. To stand in your authority isn't about false hope, misplaced trust, or wild dreams, but about the confidence of the things we have seen and heard in God. In order to really know your authority, you have to really know the one who has given it to you. Look to your circumstance, look to your situations, and see the rain. Can you hear it?

---

[29]Matthew 27:50
[30]Matthew 27: 52–53

Can you sense it coming? There is the sound of abundance of rain.

7.   *A lifestyle of authority for a lifestyle of victory*

Joshua's life was marked by victory after victory. He lived in these victories and let everything else go past him. He lived in the provision of God. Joshua didn't hang about lamenting the wasted time in the desert. He had determined in his heart, years before, that the locusts didn't need any more of his years and he lived in that. When we walk with the authority of heaven, we walk in victory. After all, the outcome is already determined and the battle is already won.

We are called to be a people who live in authority, who walk out the precious deposit entrusted to us. The psalmist writes, *"You shall tread upon the lion and the cobra, the young lion and the serpent you shall trample underfoot."* (Psalm 91: 13). We like the promise of the psalm, but we miss its real meaning sometimes. These animals do not present themselves at our feet with signs saying, '*Trample me, please.*' We come across these animals in the jungle as they stalk their prey and look to savage us. It's then with the full authority of heaven that we step with confidence and cry victory. We are not pawns in some crazy safari, we are pioneers gifted with every necessary weapon to advance the kingdom of God. It is time to stand in our authority, walk in our authority, and grow in our authority.

CHAPTER 14

A Man of Victory

Joshua's life is marked out by victory, by winning battles and establishing the Israelites in the Promised Land. It provides a marked contrast to the book it precedes, the book of Judges. Judges sees the Israelites lurching from disaster to disaster, and rescued only when they come back to a place of obedience.

What does it mean to live a life of victory? We long sometimes for a ministry, for a walk that sees the battles won, lives transformed, miracles occurring and we pray in frustration wondering why things don't seem to change. People look for formulas, study scripture, pray longer, pray louder and seek the 'all elusive' key. The life of Joshua suggests to me a simple (but difficult!) principle of obedience. Sometimes we can think we are living in a place of obedience when all we are actually doing is paying lip service to the promises of God. To be obedient is not simply to agree with the promises of God, but to be grounded in the promises of God, to live daily in His word and in the power that gives us. To be obedient is not simply to recognise the prophetic word/voice of God but to apply it to our lives, to take the words that are given on a Sunday and in our meetings and ask daily how they apply to our lives and how we live in them. To be obedient is not just to simply tithe. Tithing is just the start! Our tithe belongs to God, what we give as an offering is plus the tithe and we give it with a cheerful heart (ouch!). To be obedient is not to simply go to church but to **be** church, to stand and serve and receive in the covenant of God's people. Some people are very good at receiving and miss the blessing and relationship of serving. Some people are very good at serving but deny other people the blessing of serving when they are unable to receive. To be obedient is not just to hold to the values the Bible teaches on family life but to live them, to love your wife as Christ loved the church, to submit to your husband as to the Lord, to train and discipline your children but not exasperate them![31] We use the word obedience too quickly sometimes, true obedience is something much deeper and when we live in that place it is then that we see amazing victory.

Joshua 11 and 12 show the extent of Joshua's victory over his enemies, and also his obedience as he is called to stand and show amazing faith. Let's look at some of the principles of obedience that contribute to Joshua's victory:

1.   Obedience when it doesn't look like victory!

What did Joshua see when he looked out at the army of their enemies?[32] This was no bedraggled collection of troops but this was a multitude of soldiers, so many that they could not be counted, a united force determined to conquer the Israelites. This didn't look like a place of victory, it looked like a pretty desperate place and it certainly didn't look like they were about to win the battle. The place of obedience does not always look like the place of victory, it doesn't always seem to make sense, but know this, that in obedience to the voice of God, the hand of God will move. What do you see when you stand in your circumstances, in obedience and look for the impossible victory?

Take a moment to read the story of Elisha and the Arameans in 2 Kings 6:8–23; this passage is a powerful testimony to the victory of obedience. I love this story and every time I read it, it makes me laugh. I imagine the servant looking out of the window, seeing the army surrounding the house and wondering how on earth they are going to get out of this one! When Elisha looks he sees something totally different,

---

[31]Ephesians 5: 22–6:4
[32]Joshua 11:1–5

he sees the armies of heaven poised and ready, so much so that Elisha's initial prayer is simply *"O Lord, open his [his servants] eyes so that he may see."*[33] Elisha saw heavens answer beyond earth's problems; the victory was never in doubt because he understood that God was about to do something amazing. He was looking for the angels before he saw them.

It is easy sometimes to look back and identify victory in our lives, but what about looking forward and identifying the victory there? Let me ask you again: what do you see? I believe that part of the reason why Joshua saw such amazing things was that he positioned himself in the place of obedience and expected the miracles. He understood that when he stood in total surrender that heaven moved in awesome power.

Look with me at Acts 12: 1–19, here we have Peter's miraculous escape from prison. Peter had been thrown into prison because of his key role in the early church; he was in prison because of his obedience to the plans and purposes of God. What amazes me about this story is that we find Peter asleep.[34] Peter rested in his circumstance in the awfulness of prison, Peter slept in the intervention of heaven. His mindset was so far above his circumstance that when his release happened, he thought he was seeing a vision.[35] Know that it is still the place of victory even when the storm wrecks its havoc, the miracle is just around the corner.

2.   *Obedience to the instruction of God*

Living in victory means that we live in a place of instruction and not a place of fear. In Joshua 11: 6, God says to Joshua *"Do not be afraid of them, because by this time tomorrow I will hand all of them over to Israel, slain. You are to hamstring their horses and burn their chariots."* In other

---

[33]2 Kings 6: 17
[34]Acts 12:6
[35]Acts 12:9

words ... *"Don't worry, remember what I have already done and what I have promised to do, this is a place of victory."*[36] Joshua allowed his place of fear to become a place of instruction. For God to tell Joshua not to be afraid he must have been fearful, notice that God doesn't condemn Joshua's fear but overrides his concern with instruction. God does not dismiss our fears but provides instruction for us to move in spite of them. What do we do with our fears? When we bring our fears under God there is release and instruction but if we stay in the place of fear, that becomes our prison. Joshua moved in spite of his fear, he moved in obedience, confident that God would provide the answer. To be afraid isn't wrong, it is often a natural response, and it is what we do with that fear that matters. Joshua took a hold of his fear and marched out to fight, this is a principle that we can live by, that we recognise our fears yet we march out in our authority against the things that come against us.

Isaiah writes, *"When the enemy comes in like a flood, the Spirit of the Lord will lift up a standard against him."*[37] In the place of obedience, when we feel afraid we can look with confidence for the standard of the Lord.

3.   Obedience to promises from a long time ago

That which God has promised he is faithful to deliver, even though sometimes we have to wait a long time. In Joshua 11, we see that four times the promises that God gave to Moses are mentioned and, as a consequence, Joshua's actions as the fulfillment of these promises.[38] What God has promised he will accomplish. Peter writes that *"With the Lord a day is like a thousand years, and a thousand years are like a day. The Lord is not slow in keeping his promise, as some un-*

---

[36]My paraphrase Joshua 11: 6
[37]Isaiah 59:19b NKJV
[38]Joshua 11: 12, 15, 20 and 23

derstand slowness."[39] God is faithful to that which He has said He will do. Are there promises over your life for which you have never seen fulfillment? Know that God is faithful and that his word endures, his prophecy endures and stands the test of time. Joshua had to wait years in the wilderness before he saw the fulfillment of the prophecy he had heard in his youth, yet, many of his generation fell away because they wanted the promise without the obedience. What are the promises of God over your life? What is the word of God over your life? When it looks like everything conspires against the things that God has promised, remember that the fulfillment of the promise is the miracle. Sarah was barren, she had lived with barrenness and all that meant for years, she was past the point that she could ever physically have a child and still God fulfilled his word.

God's timing is not too early for us to deal with us or too late for us to appreciate—it is perfect. I love Caleb's attitude in Joshua 14: 10–15 when he declares, *"I have waited and waited for this promise, I may be eight-five but I am ready, ready to take the land and ready to fight, give me my promise."*[40] Caleb had lived in the promise that he would possess the land for forty years and he was ready. I don't believe that Caleb lived wishing away time, nor did he live in bitterness. He lived each day looking to that promise, so that when he had the fulfillment of it, he knew how to be in it. The promises of God are there for our encouragement, for our guidance, they are not there to snare us or cause us to be bitter. To live in a promise of a spouse is to pray for that person, to be ready for that person. To live in the promise of a child is to prepare to be a parent, to stand in faith when it seems impossible, to undertake a journey that ends with a beautiful blessing. Promises of God are not there to torment us but to release to us the answers of what God wants to do.

---

[39] 2 Peter 3: 8–9
[40] My paraphrase, Joshua 14: 10–15

Every word that God has spoken comes back with fruit. Isaiah writes that *"My word that goes out from my mouth, it will not return to me empty, but will accomplish what I desire and achieve the purpose for which I sent it."*[41] We can live in the confidence of unfulfilled promises because we know that God will do. It is time to remind God of the words that hang over our lives, not because God has forgotten, but because we need to grapple with them again.

4.   Obedience to God's plan

In Joshua 11 we see Joshua walking out God's plan at every step of the way. After the initial fight there follows a campaign to establish the authority of the Israelites throughout the land, Joshua 11: 16–23 shows how they kept fighting in accordance with what God said. Obedience to God isn't just about the start of a journey but about the journey as a whole. I remember doing orienteering as part of my PE lessons at high school. We were given a map and various instructions and sent to a big, local park to find checkpoints and collect information. My group were not particularly good at map reading so we decided instead that would look for the checkpoints (red kites) and try and do it that way, this seemed a good idea to start with but we soon became confused and missed several checkpoints—we certainly were not the wining team! We had taken the initial information and run with that and our own ideas. The combination wasn't a great success, we got some of it right, made some of it up, and missed some of it totally, resulting in an answer that was wrong. We can be like that sometimes with God, we receive an instruction and then charge on, missing out vital checkpoints and then wondering why we end up confused. When God told Noah to build him an ark, God didn't just say he wanted a big boat. He gave him a detailed plan.[42]

---

[41]Isaiah 55:11

[42]Genesis 6

God's plans have an order; our journey within that order is a journey of obedience to heaven's instruction. What does it mean to walk a journey of obedience? Let's start with two questions: *'God what are you saying?'* and *'God how do I do that?'* We can be very good at asking these questions in isolation but we need them both together. Joshua's lifestyle is a challenge of obedience. His life is marked by listening and following God's plan. We need to come to grips with God's plan for our lives, to make sure we are cultivating time to listen to the details of his plan.

5.   *Obedience as a lifestyle*

Just take a look at Joshua 12; this is a massive list of defeated kings, a list of awesome victory. When obedience is your lifestyle you live to see amazing things. Joshua had an awesome journey. As Christians our journey should be filled with awesome encounters, we should see the hand of God at work in our families, in our work places and in our churches. In God, victory is huge. It turns earth's order on its head. 1 John 5: 4–5 says: *"Everyone born of God overcomes the world. This is the victory that has overcome the world, even our faith. Who is it that overcomes the world? Only he who believes that Jesus is the Son of God."* When we live a lifestyle of obedience we live a lifestyle that overcomes the world and that stands against the enemies schemes and sees heavens victory. Obedience as a lifestyle means that we make lifestyle choices, that we choose to stand in obedience to the word of God at every turn, and that we choose to believe the promises of God over our lives. We expect to see heaven move as we stand in that place of obedience.

As you look at your life can you really say that you stand in obedience? Are you grappling with the plans and purposes of God for your life? Are you seeking Him for the detail? Is obedience your lifestyle choice? To see the things you long to see are you ready to surrender?

Before the Victory

I saw the army,
as numerous as grains of sand on the seashore,
standing grim and determined,
ready for war.

And I stilled my soul,
I listened for His voice,
which spoke to me of strategy,
and prophecies and victory,

and so my spirit lifted,
And my soul, my soul rejoiced.

CHAPTER 15

A Man Full of Years

*"Now fear the Lord and serve him with all faithful-
ness. Throw away the gods your forefathers worshipped beyond the River and in Egypt, and serve
the Lord. But if serving the Lord seems undesirable
to you, then choose for yourselves this day whom
you will serve, whether the gods your forefathers
served beyond the River, or the gods of the Amorites,
in whose land you are living. But as for me and my
household, we will serve the Lord."*

Joshua 24:14–15

Joshua was under no illusions, he knew he was going to die
and he understood that this was the end.[43] I can imagine
Joshua, a man of one hundred and ten, looking like he was
sixty and preaching this last message with both excitement
and seriousness. He was ready to die and I imagine a part of
him that simply longed to be with God, but he knew what
he was leaving behind, he knew what the Israelites were like
and he wanted to make sure he left a legacy.

I remember my last day at Morecambe High School, a
school where I had taught music for two years. I was excited
to be leaving, I had plans and projects mapped out for the
future, but I was sad at the thought of leaving behind my
colleagues. It is tradition at Morecambe High for the person
leaving to make a speech and for the head to say a few words.
I had thought and prayed carefully about what I wanted to
say, because I wanted to leave a deposit behind. I wanted
my last words to that school to be something of value. As

---

[43] Joshua 23: 2

Christians we walk through different seasons of different things God has for us, the way we leave each season is important. When we prepare to leave a season in the right way, we find that we enter the next season from a place of peace and order. As I stumbled over my speech that day, giving out what I felt God had laid on my heart, I was so blessed, unprepared for the beautiful response that met me and touched by the speech that was given about me. The order for the next academic year seemed to come together with ease as I prepared to step into the next season.

Joshua had seen how Moses left his season, he had heard Moses specific direction to him, heard the song of the spirit, witnessed Moses blessing and prophecy to the tribes, and saw him climb the mountain.[44] Moses died a strong man, the Bible says that, *"his eyes were not weak nor his strength gone."*[45] Both Moses and Joshua were old men, they had the bodies of old men but they had spirits like young men, spirits that leapt ahead.

I remember a man called Ernie. He became a Christian in his eighties and was eager to be baptised, I think he was actually around ninety when he was baptised. He climbed down into the baptistery in his shorts and t-shirt and went down under the water. As he came out of the water, we started to sing a hymn. Ernie climbed slowly out of the tank and stood by the side of the baptistery, dripping wet, eyes closed, hands outstretched, praising God. He was an old frail man but the echo of his heart reverberated round the room, *'I'm here God, use me.'* At that moment, in the spirit, age didn't matter; he had a hold of something. Ernie died a couple of years ago now, ready to walk into a new season of praise and worship!

Sometimes seasons are difficult to stay in, sometimes seasons are difficult to leave, and we need to be a people who know how to stay and how to leave in the right way. Sometimes we don't have the answers. Hear the heart of the

---

[44]Deuteronomy 31–34
[45]Deuteronomy 34: 7b

apostle Paul as he wrestles, *"For to me, to live is Christ and to die is gain. If I am able to go on living in the body, this will mean fruitful labour for me. Yet what shall I choose? I do not know! I am torn between the two: I desire to depart and be with Christ, which is better by far; but it is more necessary for you that I remain in the body. Convinced of this, I know that I will remain, and I will continue with all of you for your progress and joy in the faith, so that through my being with you again your joy in Christ Jesus will overflow on account of me."*[46] Paul knew that God was using this season in his life, but he found it hard because he knew that there was a much better season ahead. Paul battled with death continually. In everything that was flung at him, his flesh had to fight to stay alive, Paul chose to fight because he understood that God was using this season. In every season of life that we go through, God is our strength and when we have nothing left, he meets us with the resources of heaven. Isaiah writes: *"Even youths grow tired and weary and young men stumble and fall; but those who hope in the Lord will renew their strength. They will soar on wings like eagles; they will run and not grow weary, they will walk and not be faint."*[47]

God is the lifter of our head, the author of every season and, just as he directs the start of every season, he shows us the end. The start of Joshua's season was very clear, there was a word that simply said: *"Moses my servant is dead."*[48] The end of Joshua's season was also very clear, the last chapters of Joshua show him putting things in order, he didn't leave chaos – he dispelled the chaos that could potentially take over.

The last two chapters of Joshua leave the Israelites with very clear instructions, Joshua is determined that they will stay on the right path, that they won't be led astray. Joshua 24: 1—14 is a catalogue of remembrance, a cry from the

---

[46]Philippians 1: 21–24
[47]Isaiah 40: 28
[48]Joshua 1: 2

heart of Joshua, '*remember what the Lord has done.*' In these verses, the Israelites are reminded that God has made them into a nation. His miracle power brought them out of captivity, fought for them, protected them from false prophets and provided for them.[49] If ever the Israelites are tempted by anything else, they just need to look at what God has done. The same is true for us, when we are faced with temptation we need to look at our testimony. Every time I share my testimony, or look back over what God has done, it amazes me; it sparks a spirit of gratitude inside my heart that inspires praise. When Joshua tells the Israelites to remember, he doesn't just stop with things in living memory, he goes right back to Abraham, as if he is saying to the Israelites, '*remember who you are.*' Our testimony goes back to the cross; we remember what Jesus did for us. Our testimony goes right back to the fact that Jesus himself prayed for us, John 17: 20—26, our testimony is of resurrection power.

When Joshua calls out for the Israelites to remember, he is looking for something that will imprint on their hearts, something that will resonate every time they try and rebel. When we look back on our testimony, we look back with victory, it isn't meant to make us sad. I imagine Joshua speaking out these verses with real encouragement, the fire dancing in his eyes as he says: '*remember.*' There is another way that Joshua could have told this story, he could have focused on the death in the wilderness or even the disobedience that kept the Israelites wandering, but that wasn't the object of the exercise. The call of remembrance was a call to remember God's power.

Joshua also speaks to the people about the present, the now that they are living in. In Joshua 23: 12–13, Joshua is very clear, he commands the people not to intermarry. He gets the people to look at where they are and see what's around them, to be aware of what will happen if they make mistakes. In order to enter a new season, we have to be aware

---

[49]Joshua 24: 1–14

of the surroundings we are in. We don't just dance into new
things with ignorance; ignorance is not always bliss and is
sometimes very dangerous. God wants us to be a people who
are aware and are discerning. It could have seemed like a
nice thing to do, coming alongside other nations, sharing
their Jewishness with other cultures, but God knows best.
When God says no he is making sure that His people stay on
the right path, He knows that if the Israelites had gotten too
close to other religions, things would have gone very wrong,
very quickly. We can't go into a new season in oblivion, we
go in with supernatural sight; otherwise, things that can look
good can end up being a snare.

As well as encouraging the people to remember their testimony and to be aware of the present, Joshua also encour-
ages the people to see the prophetic.[50] Joshua knows that to
advance you need to hear and act on the voice of God. There
is an exhortation in Joshua 23: 5 to keep fighting, Joshua
knows that the battles aren't finished yet, the outcome is decided, but the land is still to be taken. We need to understand
what the prophetic words are over our lives in order to run
with them effectively. If the Israelites could get a handle on
the fact that *"One of you routs a thousand, because the Lord
fights for you,"*[51] they would be invincible! In charismatic
churches, we can be very good at receiving prophetic words,
encouraging people to bring prophetic words, and do less
well at grappling with these words and walking them out. It
is time not just to receive the prophetic, but also to walk out
the prophetic.

As Joshua prepares to leave the people, he leaves them
with a choice. Having preached his sermon, (Joshua 24:
1–14) he leaves them with something that they have con-
fessed and that they will remember. In Joshua 24: 15 there
is a challenge: *'choose'*—Joshua wants to hear their confession, he wants them to hear their own confession, he

---

[50]Joshua 23: 4, 5 and 10
[51]Joshua 23: 10

challenges their initial confession with a provocation *"You are not able to serve the Lord. He is a holy God; he is a jealous God."*[52] In other words *"Don't just say yes, think about your yes, this is your life, this is your future."* This makes me think of Peter when Jesus reinstates him,[53] Jesus asks Peter the same question three times *"Do you love me?"* I wonder how Peter felt when Jesus asked him the same question; I believe Peter knew that Jesus was looking for a deeper response. Not just the *'yes'* but the *'yes.'* Words are not meant to be cheap but we can cheapen them if we are not careful. If you look at Peter's third response you can see a difference, there is almost a resignation in Peter's answer but also the recognition that the type of love and devotion that Jesus is after is not just a *'friendship'* love but an *'all consuming love.'* His answer mirrors the response that he gives as he is effectively told that he will be martyred for his faith. To say yes to Jesus is a serious thing, it is life changing, and in every yes there is something that changes our lives again. It is time to understand what it means to say yes to heaven.

For the Israelites, after they had said yes there was a very clear instruction, *"throw away the foreign gods that are among you and yield your hearts to the Lord."*[54] In other words *'get rid of all your distractions, everything that sets itself up against me and come under my rule.'* Notice that the throwing away comes first If you try and submit to God, and still pursue things that are not of God, you will wind up very frustrated, you can't run opposite ways at the same time. To throw away something is not to pass it on but to count it as rubbish and see it destroyed, only when we have thrown away our rubbish do we yield to God's rule.

To yield is to give as fruit or gain, or result, to surrender or allow access, to yield is to be forced out of your natural

---

[52]Joshua 23: 19
[53]See John 21: 15–20
[54]Joshua 24:23

shape. Just think about that for a minute—when we say to God, 'I yield my heart', what we are saying is, *'I give my life as fruit for your kingdom, my gain for your glory, my abilities and talents so that others are drawn to you, I surrender all that I am, I allow you access to every area of my life, you can use me as you want to, bend me to your plans and purpose and to your will, I prefer your way.'* Notice God does not say yield your words, but yield your heart, your very lifeblood, your every plan, and your every desire.

There is a beautiful old chorus that we used to sing called 'Pierce my Ear,' it goes like this:

> Pierce my ear, O Lord my God
> Take me to your throne this day,
> I will serve no other God,
> Lord, I'm here to stay.[55]

In Bible times, a slave could choose to stay with his Master after he had earned his freedom. If a slave chose to stay, even after he could have had his freedom, his master would take him and pierce his ear, he would wear that earring all his life. The heart cry of this song is a heart cry of surrender; it is a picture of a yielded heart.

For the Israelites, Joshua gave them a memorial. Joshua provided the people with two memorials, a written memorial and a visual memorial.[56] Every time the Israelites read the Law of God they would find reference to that day and, every time they saw this large stone, they would be reminded that they had decided to yield to God. What was written on that book could not be erased and I doubt that anyone in living memory of the memorial tried to move that stone. When we lay markers down it is good to lay a memorial down, something that ties that decision to something concrete. A

---

[55]"Pierce my Ear," Steve Croft 1980 Dayspring Music, LLC
[56]Joshua 24: 24–26

few months back I composed a song called: 'Healer'—the opening verse states:

> You are my healer,
> You are my confidence,
> You are my hope,
> You make me strong,
> You are my answer,
> You're my provider,
> You are my life,
> You are my song.[57]

This song was not written because God had healed me. When I composed this song I didn't feel well, I wasn't healed. I composed this song out of a decision to yield my heart to God's purpose for my life; it was a supernatural declaration of faith that God would heal me. This song is a memorial to a time when I decided to think differently, it serves as a reminder to me of the decision I made. When we sing it in church it catches me, it reminds me, and it challenges me. Memorials are not just nice places of remembrance but powerful places of right confession that inform our choices when we catch sight of them. What memorials do we allow to inform our choices?

As we come to the end of Joshua's life, we see a man ready to go into glory, looking forward with excitement to what God has. Joshua is a man that speaks a prophetic legacy over his household, declaring *"as for me and my household, we will serve the Lord."*[58] What do we declare over our households? Joshua knew he was about to die, he knew he wouldn't be around. That declaration was a declaration to his wife, his sons and daughters, his grandchildren, and his great-grandchildren. It was a prophetic confession designed

---

[57]Song, "Healer" by Beckie Jo Snell 2009, Kings Community Church, Lancaster, England.
[58]Joshua 24: 15b

to roar through the generations, a confession that shouted to the heavenly realms, *'my children belong to God, their children belong to God, and their children's children belong to God.'* Joshua understood the favour of the Lord; he had listened to Moses teaching and he knew the power of obedience.[59] He had grasped hold of the fact that, when he yielded his heart totally to God, he could expect amazing things to happen. God is looking for a people who shout out over their households—*'me and my household, we will!'* I look at my own family, many of whom don't know Jesus and my heart breaks, but I know God can move. Notice Joshua doesn't shout out *'me and my family,'* but *'me and my household'*— i.e., everything I own, all my money, my livestock, and my ability. It is time to extend our shout out, that out of a yielded heart we declare salvation over our households. It can be too easy sometimes to shout out frustration over our households when what is needed is a word, the disturbance of a yielded heart that cries, *'me and my household.'*

Notice that Joshua starts with 'me,' that he knows it begins with him. For Joshua, that 'me' was a comment on his life, a comment on his testimony. He knew he was going on, he was shouting out of what God had already done. The shout starts with our obedience, our walk, and then out of that comes the intercession for our households, a roar that covers generations.

For Joshua, he finished his life buried in the land of his inheritance;[60] he finished his life in the right position. He died knowing that he had fulfilled God's plan for his life, the Bible says that:

> *"After these things, Joshua son of Nun, the servant of the Lord, died at the age of a hundred and ten. And they buried him in the land of his inheritance, at Timnath Serah in the hill country of Ephraim, north*

---

[59]Deuteronomy 28
[60]Joshua 24:29

of Mount Gaash. Israel served the Lord throughout the lifetime of Joshua and of the elders who outlived him and who had experienced everything the Lord had done for Israel."

Joshua 24: 29–31

This was a man who left a powerful legacy and who established Israel in the place of their inheritance. What an epitaph to have!

As we come to the end of this book, can I encourage you to look again at where you are? Time does not stand still. God restores to us the years that the locusts have devoured and he is always faithful, but we stand accountable for the choices we make. I want to be buried in the land of my inheritance. I want to leave a legacy that draws people closer to God, I want to see salvation, but it starts with my choice, my approach, and obedience in the season that God has placed me in. When I look at my life now, what am I leaving? What is my legacy?

CONCLUSION

Recapture Your Dream

"Then Joshua sent the people away, each to his own inheritance."

Joshua 24: 28

Look at your inheritance again. Where has God put you? What is His purpose in this season? Where is your inheritance? 1 Peter 1: 3–6 talks about an inheritance that doesn't fade away but lasts, that endures with us through our trials. The desert is a very real place, and not a nice one, but in that desert place we can still live with the mindset of inheritance. Joshua walked through the desert but he never inhabited that place, those who inhabited the desert place died there. Joshua chose instead to inhabit the prophetic word of God, the promises that God had given to him. Joshua never lost his dream of seeing the Promised Land, he lived for that day, and he expected that he would live to see that day; he understood God's heart for him, he knew in his spirit he would see that land. When we choose to come out of the desert, we are choosing a mindset. The desert is still the desert until the miracle power of God changes it, but in the desert place we can live in the excitement of the prophetic and the promise.

God is looking for a heart that says simply 'yes.' Joshua's journey started when he aligned himself with men of God, people who shared his heart. I can really imagine him and Caleb coming back with the spoils of the land, working out how to manoeuvre this pole of fruit out of enemy territory without being seen, laughing with the confidence that this was their land.[61] They went looking for fruit, looking for the

---

[61]Numbers 13

139

good things, not looking at the enemy; they understood that the battle was already won. We need that same spirit, a spirit that looks at problems with the eyes of heaven and sees the answer before it is even there.

It is time to recapture your dreams. God given dreams are not meant to languish away in journals but be seen in all their glory. The Promised Land hasn't gone anywhere; the answers of heaven are always the answers of heaven. Look past the desert, past the problems, through the battle, into the prophetic, towards the victory, past your mistakes, over the disappointment of people who have let you down, and see your inheritance. Your inheritance can't be given to anybody else, it is marked out just for you, and it can't be given away.

It is time to dream again, time to roar through the generations, that *'me and my household will serve the Lord.'*[62] Change your cry of frustration to a prophetic declaration and watch what heaven will do. Understand your authority, understand who you are, spend time in the tent worshipping when everyone else has gone, allow the revelation and the strategy of heaven to pierce your heart and get ready to come and cross the Jordan. What an adventure lies before us, what a journey we anticipate as we come out of the desert!

"When you see the Covenant-Chest of God, your God, carried by the Levitical priests, start moving. Follow it. Make sure you keep a proper distance between you and it, about half a mile— be sure now to keep your distance!—and you'll see clearly the route to take. You've never been on this road before. . . . Sanctify yourselves. Tomorrow God will work miracle-wonders among you."[63]

You are never too old to dance with the energy of heaven and you are never too young to take up the mantle that God has for you. It is time to come alive to the things of God, to come out of the desert.

---

[62]Joshua 24: 15b

[63]Joshua 3: 2–5 The Message

I may not see
the bubbling streams,
the abundant vineyards that grow and grow,
with freshness and vitality,

But with every step
on this burning sand,
My heart chooses to declare
the faithfulness of God and
"I see it,"

"yes, I see it,"

"I dream it,"
"yes, I will dream it,"

I am excited
So excited,

and I'm moving.

Lightning Source UK Ltd.
Milton Keynes UK
11 March 2011

169118UK00002B/9/P